Kashif Ali studied law at the Universities of Oxford and Cambridge and has been a practising Barrister at St Johns Buildings Chambers in Manchester since 2005 specialising in employment law.

# A Practical Guide to Religion and Belief Discrimination Claims in the Workplace

# A Practical Guide to Religion and Belief Discrimination Claims in the Workplace

Kashif Ali
Barrister-at-Law
MA (Oxon), LLM (Cantab)

Law Brief Publishing

Published 2020 by Law Brief Publishing, an imprint of Law Brief Publishing Ltd
30 The Parks
Minehead
Somerset
TA24 8BT

www.lawbriefpublishing.com

Paperback: 978-1-913715-27-4

# PREFACE

This text has been written to explore the requirements and challenges of bringing workplace discrimination claims on grounds of religion and belief under the Equality Act 2010. It is hoped it will be of assistance to lawyers, law students, HR professionals and litigants in persons.

I would like to thank employment lawyers and employment judges I have worked with and appeared before over the years, and indeed continue to do so, for their assistance with my better understanding of this area of law. Of course any errors, omissions and opinions are entirely mine.

The stated guidance and law is understood to be correct and up-to-date as of 1 November 2020.

Kashif Ali
November 2020

# CONTENTS

*Abbreviations and Definitions*

Chapter One Introduction 1
1.1 Purpose of this text 1
1.2 Contextual analysis of religion and beliefs in the workplace 2
1.3 The legislative protection 3

Chapter Two Defining "Religion" 5
2.1 Legal definition of religion 5
2.2 Examples of religion 6
2.3 Determining religion in the workplace 8

Chapter Three Defining "Belief" 11
3.1 Legal definition of belief 11
3.2 Examples of beliefs 13
3.3 Determining beliefs in the workplace 16
3.4 Need for knowledge about beliefs 17

Chapter Four Who is Protected? 19
4.1 Employees 19
4.2 Job applicants 22
4.3 Former employees 23
4.4 Contract workers 25
4.5 Volunteers 26
4.6 Specific occupations 28

| | | |
|---|---|---|
| Chapter Five | Direct Discrimination | 29 |
| | 5.1 The less favourable treatment than a comparator test | 30 |
| | 5.2 The causation test | 33 |
| | 5.3 The employer's motive | 38 |
| | 5.4 Direct discrimination by association | 39 |
| | 5.5 "Permissible" direct discrimination | 40 |
| Chapter Six | Indirect Discrimination | 45 |
| | 6.1 What is the provision, criterion or practice being complained about? | 47 |
| | 6.2 Was the provision, criterion or practice applied generally? | 49 |
| | 6.3 Did the provision, criterion or practice put those who share a particular religion or belief at a particular disadvantage? | 49 |
| | 6.4 Did the provision, criterion or practice in fact put the complaining employee at a disadvantage? | 51 |
| | 6.5 Is the provision, criterion or practice justified? | 53 |
| Chapter Seven | Harassment | 63 |
| | 7.1 Identifying unwanted conduct | 64 |
| | 7.2 The causation test | 68 |
| | 7.3 Did the unwanted conduct cause offence? | 70 |
| | 7.4 Witnessing the harassment of a work colleague by another work colleague | 73 |
| | 7.5 Harassment by a third party | 73 |
| Chapter Eight | Victimisation | 75 |
| | 8.1 Subjecting the employee to a detriment | 76 |
| | 8.2 The protected act | 76 |
| | 8.3 The causation test | 78 |
| | 8.4 Victimisation by association | 79 |

| | | |
|---|---|---|
| Chapter Nine | Religious Preaching | 83 |
| Chapter Ten | Employer's Liability for Its Employees | 89 |
| | 10.1 Not in the course of employment | 91 |
| | 10.2 Reasonable steps defence | 98 |
| Chapter Eleven | Remedies for Religion or Belief Discrimination | 101 |
| | 11.1 Financial losses | 103 |
| | 11.2 Injury to feelings compensation | 104 |
| | 11.3 Personal injury compensation | 107 |
| Chapter Twelve | Concluding Remarks | 109 |

# ABBREVIATIONS AND DEFINITIONS

| | |
|---|---|
| EA 2010 | Equality Act 2010 |
| PCP | A provision, criterion or practice in the workplace |
| ET | Employment Tribunal |
| EAT | Employment Appeal Tribunal |
| CA | Court of Appeal |
| ACAS | The Advisory, Conciliation and Arbitration Service |
| ACAS Guide | ACAS Guidance on "Religion or belief discrimination: key points for the workplace" (August 2018) |
| ECHR | European Convention on Human Rights |
| HRA 1998 | Human Rights Act 1998 |

# CHAPTER ONE
# INTRODUCTION

## 1.1 Purpose of this text

The purpose of this text is both to set out the legal framework for bringing religion and belief discrimination claims in the workplace pursuant to the Equality Act 210 (the "EA 2010"), and to offer practical guidance and assistance to legal practitioners, human resources professionals, employers and employees in relation to such claims.

In Chapter 2 there is a discussion about what *religion* is, and in Chapter 3 what *beliefs* are. In Chapter 4 there is a discussion about who in the workplace is protected by the legislation. In Chapters 5-8 there is a discussion about the types of anti-discrimination legislative protection in employment law as far as religion and beliefs are concerned. In Chapter 9 there is a discussion about how employers might deal with employees who are preaching their own religious and other beliefs inappropriately in the workplace. In Chapter 10 there is a discussion about whose discriminatory actions the employer will be liable for and in what circumstances. And in Chapter 11 there is a discussion about remedies and compensation to employees in cases of discrimination on grounds of religion and belief.

The aim is to offer an overview using straight-forward language. Throughout I will try to illustrate the issues with decided cases, practical examples and available guidance.

## 1.2 Contextual analysis of religion and beliefs in the workplace

There are two related but distinct focuses as far as religion and belief in the workplace is concerned.

First, the *anti-discrimination* focus. In a nutshell this is concerned with preventing the discrimination of employees on grounds of their religion or beliefs. On the face of it this is the pre-occupation of the EA 2010 and what it seeks to do.

Straight-forward examples of discrimination might include: refusing to employ someone because they are Jewish; enforcing a strict dress code so as to effectively exclude from your organisation Sikhs who wear turbans; tolerating Islamaphobic banter on the factory floor to the extent that a Muslim employee feels harassed; or taking overtime away from a Christian employee to punish them for having complained about working on Sundays.

Second, the *religious liberty* focus. The concern here is not so much with preventing the discrimination of employees on grounds of their religion or beliefs but instead with allowing them to express their religion or beliefs. Ideas interwoven with liberal democracies include allowing the free practice of religion (see for example Article 9 of the ECHR which guarantees the right to freedom of thought, conscience and religion). And there is a social pressure and growing recognition that people should be able to express themselves and their individual identities in all elements of their life. It is unrealistic to expect people to park religious and belief identities at the door of the workplace. And just as the anti-discrimination focus is supported in law with the EA 2010, there is some limited support for the religious liberty focus in legislation too. Section 3 of the HRA 1998 places an interpretative obligation on courts and tribunals to read all legislation (including workplace employment legislation) as far as possible in a way compatible with ECHR rights.

Simple examples in the workplace might include: offering time off work to a Jewish employee to celebrate Rosh Hashanah even if it falls at a time of year when holidays are not usually permitted such as term time; having a designated prayer room for Muslim employees to pray during the day; and allowing a Christian employee to wear a cross or a Sikh employee to wear a kara.

It's the author's view that these two focusses, though in theory distinct, in practice are interwoven and inescapably connected for the purposes of the workplace. The practical issues this raises are far from straight-forward. For example, if your staff canteen offers halal food options, you will undoubtedly be seen as an employer accommodating your Muslim employees. But if you do not offer halal food options are you discriminating against your Muslim employees? Does it make a difference if only 5% of your workforce is Muslim as compared to 50% of your workforce being Muslim? If you are providing halal food options in the canteen, then are your discriminating against others by say not providing kosher or vegan options?

## 1.3 The legislative protection

In 2000 the European Union enacted the Employment Framework Council Directive 2000/78/EC which provided at Article 1: "The purpose of this Directive is to lay down a general framework for combating discrimination on the grounds of religion or belief, disability, age or sexual orientation as regards employment and occupation, with a view to putting into effect in the Member States the principle of equal treatment". Article 18 required Member States to introduce the necessary national domestic legislation to further the objectives of the Directive by 2 December 2003.

In response the UK Government introduced the Employment Equality (Religion or Belief) Regulations 2003. These sought to prohibit direct discrimination, indirect discrimination, harassment and victimisation on grounds of religion and beliefs.

The EA 2010 consolidated and enhanced existing anti-discrimination legislation and now contains all the relevant provisions.

Section 4 of the EA 2010 lists the nine protected characteristics of which "religion or belief" is just one. The others are: age; disability; gender reassignment; marriage and civil partnership; pregnancy and maternity; race; sex; and sexual orientation.

Section 10 of the EA 2010 defines "religion" and "belief". What "religion" and "belief" mean and how they are interpreted is explored more fully in Chapters 2 and 3 of this text.

Part 2 Chapters 2 and 5 of the EA 2010 set out the areas of prohibited discriminatory conduct in the workplace. In simple terms the following four types of conduct are prohibited under the EA 2010:

1. Direct discrimination contrary to section 13.
2. Indirect discrimination contrary to section 19.
3. Harassment contrary to section 26.
4. Victimisation contrary to section 27.

These types of discrimination are explained and discussed further below.

# CHAPTER TWO
# DEFINING "RELIGION"

## 2.1 Legal definition of religion

"Religion" is not comprehensively or clearly defined in the EA 2010. Section 10(1) rather unhelpfully defines "religion" as follows:

> "Religion means any religion and a reference to religion includes a reference to a lack of religion."

The Explanatory Notes to the EA 2010[1] provide:

> "This section defines the protected characteristic of religion or religious or philosophical belief, which is stated to include for this purpose a lack of religion or belief. It is a broad definition in line with the freedom of thought, conscience and religion guaranteed by Article 9 of the European Convention on Human Rights. The main limitation for the purposes of Article 9 is that the religion must have a clear structure and belief system. Denominations or sects within a religion can be considered to be a religion or belief, such as Protestants and Catholics within Christianity."

The ACAS Guide[2] offers the following five-point guidance on the definition of "religion" under the EA 2010:

1. A religion must have a clear structure and belief system.

---

1 At Section 10 at paragraph 51

2 ACAS Guidance on "Religion or belief discrimination: key points for the workplace" (August 2018) at page 4

2. A clearly structured denomination or sect within a religion can be covered.

3. Employees without a religious faith, as well as those with a faith, are protected. Someone who is not a Hindu would be protected against discrimination because "they are not a Hindu".

4. What makes up religious belief or practice may vary among people in that religion.

5. No one religion or branch of a religion overrides another – so an employee is protected against discrimination by someone of another religion, or of the same religion or of a different branch or practice of their religion. For example, it would be discriminatory for an employee to treat a colleague of the same religion unfairly because they regard them as less orthodox in their belief.

## 2.2 Examples of religion

The major religions of the world would certainly be included:

- Baha'i
- Buddhism
- Christianity
- Confucianism
- Hinduism

- Islam
- Jainism
- Judaism
- Rastafarianism
- Shinto
- Sikhism
- Taoism
- Zoroastrianism

Indeed, examples are given in the Explanatory Notes to the EA 2010[3] are: "The Baha'i faith, Buddhism, Christianity, Hinduism, Islam, Jainism, Judaism, Rastafarianism, Sikhism and Zoroastrianism are all religions for the purposes of this provision."

Most religions of course have subdivisions.

- Hindu subdivisions include Vaishnavism, Shaivism, Shaktism and Smartism.
- Christians for example might identify as Roman Catholic, Protestant, Eastern Orthodox, Greek Orthodox, Anglican, or Methodist.
- Muslims might be Sunni, Shia, Ibadi, Ahmadi or Sufi.

---

3 At Section 10 at paragraph 53

- Jews can be ultra-Orthodox, Orthodox, Conservative, Reform for example.
- Buddhism includes Theravāda and Mahayana which then have their own subdivisions.

The focus should not be solely on the main religions of the world and their sub-divisions, and less well-known localised religions from the different corners of the world may also qualify for protection, such as many traditional African religions[4].

Finally, new religions can arise or attempts to recognise new religions can occur. For example, albeit in a different context, in 2016 the Temple of the Jedi Order (members of which follow the tenets of the faith central to the Star Wars films) failed to be recognised as a religious organisation under UK charity law[5].

## 2.3 Determining religion in the workplace

Employers should have in mind the following additional points when determining religion and issues of religious discrimination in the workplace.

First, employees may self-identify the religion they belong to differently depending on the context. So an employee may self-describe their religion as "Muslim" for the purposes of requesting time off for Eid festivities, but describe themselves as "Sunni" to describe harassment from a Shi'ite colleague.

---

4 https://thebestschools.org/magazine/world-religions-study-starters/#traditional-african

5 https://www.theguardian.com/society/2016/dec/19/temple-of-the-jedi-order-application-religion-rejected-charity-commission-uk

Second, it is not at all uncommon for employees to complain about religious discrimination from people who belong to the same religion. Employers should be careful not to assume there cannot be religious discrimination between two employees because they are of the same religion. For example:

- A Jewish business owner may mistreat a Jewish employee unfairly because of her decision to date non-Jewish men.
- A Christian manager may mistreat a Christian co-worker because he was not joining him for Sunday prayers.

Thirdly, as the ACAS Guide[6] makes clear that not all followers of a particular religion will necessarily make the same requests. Levels of adherence to a religion, or beliefs concerning that religion can vary. Practices can vary amongst individuals. Muslims may practice the Eid festival on different days. Some Christians may require time off over the Easter period, others may not make any request for time off at Easter. Employers should very importantly keep this in mind, and not make assumptions about religion or religious faith and practices.

It is also important to bear in mind that some employees are more private and discreet about religion than others.

And further people can change the level and their style of devotion or worship over time. An employee may become more or less devout. Adherence to a religion or belief is not static. People can even change their religious views entirely and convert into different faiths.

---

6 ACAS Guidance on "Religion or belief discrimination: key points for the workplace" (August 2018) at page 13

# CHAPTER THREE
# DEFINING "BELIEF"

### 3.1 Legal definition of belief

An employer must not discriminate against an employee on grounds of their "belief". It is therefore important for employers to understand which beliefs are protected under the EA 2010 and which are not.

Section 10(2) of the EA 2010 defines "belief" as follows:

> "Belief means any religious or philosophical belief and a reference to belief includes a reference to a lack of belief."

The Explanatory Notes to the EA 2010 provide[1]:

> "The criteria for determining what is a "philosophical belief" are that it must be genuinely held; be a belief and not an opinion or viewpoint based on the present state of information available; be a belief as to a weighty and substantial aspect of human life and behaviour; attain a certain level of cogency, seriousness, cohesion and importance; and be worthy of respect in a democratic society, compatible with human dignity and not conflict with the fundamental rights of others. So, for example, any cult involved in illegal activities would not satisfy these criteria".

1 At Section 10 at paragraph 52

Further in the Explanatory Notes it is stated[2]: “Beliefs such as humanism and atheism would be beliefs for the purposes of this provision but adherence to a particular football team would not be”.

On the basis of the Explanatory Notes the ACAS Guide[3] offers the following five-point guidance on how a “philosophical belief” could be determined. It must be all of the following:

1. genuinely held
2. not just an opinion or point-of-view based on current information
3. a weighty and substantial aspect of human life and behaviour
4. clear, logical, convincing, serious, important and
5. worthy of respect in a democratic society, compatible with human dignity and not conflict with the fundamental rights of others.

The ACAS Guide[4] further advises that it is broadly accepted that supporting a political party is not a philosophical belief under the EA 2020, however a political philosophy affecting significantly how a person lives their life may be protected.

One of the leading cases is *Grainger Plc v Nicholson*[5]. The EAT explained that to qualify as a "philosophical belief", the belief had to satisfy the following criteria: it had to (i) be genuinely held; (ii) be a

2 At Section 10 at paragraph 53

3 ACAS Guidance on “Religion or belief discrimination: key points for the workplace” (August 2018) at page 5

4 As above

5 *Grainger Plc v Nicholson* [2010] 2 All ER 253 (EAT) see especially para 24

belief and not a viewpoint or opinion based on the present state of information available; (iii) be as to a weighty substantial aspect of human life and behaviour; (iv) attain a certain level of cogency, seriousness, cohesion and importance; (v) be worthy of respect in a democratic society, and not be incompatible with the fundamental rights of others.

### 3.2 Examples of beliefs

Below are some examples of "beliefs" which would likely satisfy the definition of section 10(2) of the EA 2010:

1. A belief in man-made climate change and the alleged resulting moral imperatives[6].
2. Pacifism[7].
3. A belief in a political philosophy or doctrine, such as the political philosophies of Socialism, Marxism, Communism or free-market Capitalism[8].
4. A belief in democratic socialism[9].
5. Left-wing democratic socialist beliefs[10].

---

6 *Grainger Plc v Nicholson* [2010] 2 All ER 253 (EAT) see paras 2-3

7 *Grainger Plc v Nicholson* [2010] 2 All ER 253 (EAT) see para 27

8 *Grainger Plc v Nicholson* [2010] 2 All ER 253 (EAT) see para 28

9 *Olivier v Department for Work and Pensions* (2013) (Unreported, ET 170140/13). The employment tribunal held that the belief in "democratic socialism" held by a dismissed jobcentre worker who has long been politically active with the Labour Party is a "philosophical belief" under the Equality Act 2010.

10 *Henderson v General Municipal & Boilermakers Union* [2016] EWCA Civ 1049 see para 10

6. A belief in Scottish independence and the social democratic values of the Scottish National Party[11].

7. Philosophical beliefs which are based on science, such as Darwinism[12].

8. A belief in the sanctity of life (including a fervent anti fox-hunting belief)[13].

9. A very strong belief in personal freedom and privacy, respect for personal property, freedom from authoritarianism including in the workplace, and respect for human rights and human dignity[14].

10. Ethical veganism[15].

11. A philosophical belief in "BBC values" (specifically public service broadcasting has the higher purpose of promoting cultural interchange and social cohesion)[16].

---

11 *McEleny v Ministry of Defence* (2018) (Unreported, 25 July 2018, ET Glasgow) held that a belief in Scottish independence can be a philosophical belief under the Equality Act 2010 for the purposes of protection against discrimination.

12 *Grainger Plc v Nicholson* [2010] 2 All ER 253 (EAT) see para 30

13 *Hashman v Milton Park (Dorset) Ltd t/a Orchard Park* (2011) (ET) [Southampton Tribunal, 31.1.11, ET Case No.3105555/09]. The Claimant in the case was a lifelong animal rights activist and anti-hunt campaigner. His belief system, as described by him, was that, "people should live their lives with mindful respect for animals and we all have a moral obligation to live in a way which is kind to each other, our environment and our fellow creatures". The Tribunal concluded it was relevant that the Claimant thought very deeply about the issues arising from his beliefs and that he attempted to live his life in accord with those beliefs.

14 *Nikiel-Wolski v Burton's Foods Limited* [2013] EqLR 192

15 *Casamitjana v League Against Cruel Sports* (2020) [Unreported, 21 January 2020, ET Norwich] especially at para 39.

16 *Maistry v BBC* [2014] EWCA Civ 1116 see para 3.

12. A belief in spiritualism and life after death and psychic powers[17].

13. A belief in the ancient Greek philosophy of Stoicism[18].

And here are some examples of "beliefs" which would be unlikely to satisfy the definition of section 10(2) of the EA 2010:

1. Support for a political party[19].

2. Marxist and Trotskyist beliefs were held not to be worthy of respect in a democratic society as they involved a belief in the right of the individual to break the law to achieve political aims, and the right to deprive individuals of their homes and property[20].

3. A belief in the supreme nature of the Jedi Knights is likely to fail[21].

4. Vegetarianism was held by a Tribunal to not be about human life and behaviour but a lifestyle choice, and so it was not protected as a belief[22].

---

17 *Power v Greater Manchester Police Authority* (2010) (Unreported October 8, 2010 (EAT) HHJ Peter Clark in UKEAT/0434/09).

18 In *Samuel Jackson v Lidl* (South London ET, September 2020, Judge Simon Cheetham) the employment Tribunal agreed that Stoicism was a belief protected under the Equality Act 2000 and allowed a discrimination claim to proceed to the next stage.

19 *Grainger Plc v Nicholson* [2010] 2 All ER 253 (EAT) see para 28.

20 *Kelly and others v Unison* (2009) ET/2203854/08

21 *Grainger Plc v Nicholson* [2010] 2 All ER 253 (EAT) see para 28.

22 *Conisbee v Crossley Farms Ltd* & Others (2019) [Unreported, 6 September 2019, ET Norwich] especially at paras 39-40.

5. Gender critical opinions that sex is immutable, whatever a person's stated gender identity or gender expression[23].

6. The belief in the right to own copyright (specifically the statutory human or moral right to own the copyright and moral rights of her own creative works and output, except when that creative work or output is produced on behalf of an employer)[24].

7. A belief that a global elite was seeking to establish a New World Order (a secret satanic ideology to enslave the masses and claim control of the world's resources)[25].

### 3.3 Determining beliefs in the workplace

What the above definitions and case law examples demonstrate is that the same belief in two people may lead to two different results in terms of whether it is a protected "belief" under the EA 2010 or not. Whether someone's belief in an individual case is protected depends on all the circumstances of a case, the importance of that belief to the

---

23 *Forstater v CGD Europe* [2019] 12 WLUK 516 (ET). The claimant posted tweets expressing her concerns about the proposed changes to the Gender Recognition Act 2004 which would allow people to self-identify their gender; stated that sex was binary; that trans women were men and trans men were women; and that she would continue to use what she deemed were the appropriate pronouns for people. The Tribunal found that the claimant's belief was incompatible with human dignity and the fundamental rights of others.

24 *Gray v Mulberry Co (Design) Ltd* [2019] EWCA Civ 1720 see paras 26-29. The Court of Appeal held that a belief in "the statutory human or moral right to own the copyright and moral rights of her own creative works and output, except when that creative work or output is produced on behalf of an employer" was not protected.

25 *Farrell v South Yorkshire Police Authority* [2011] EqLR 935 (ET/2803805/10)

person concerned, and how the belief affects how that person lives his or her life.

This makes it rather difficult for an employer or employee to fairly determine which beliefs would qualify for protection under the EA 2010.

### 3.4 Need for knowledge about beliefs

Unsurprisingly it has been clarified by the Courts that an employer was not motivated to discriminate against an employee because of the employee's philosophical belief where they did not know about that belief.

The case of *Maistry v BBC*[26] concerned an employee M who was a journalist employed by the BBC. He was dismissed on grounds of poor performance. He complained that the real reason for his dismissal was his philosophical belief in "BBC values". M gave evidence about his belief that public service broadcasting had a higher purpose of cultural interchange, social cohesion and debating important issues. The judge accepted that M had a genuine and strongly held belief in public service broadcasting and that his belief in BBC values was a protected belief. However M's claim failed because he had never articulated his beliefs to his employer, and so their actions could not have been motivated by or because of his beliefs.

Similarly, in *Harris v NKL Automotive Ltd*[27], the EAT accepted that a direct discrimination claim was bound to fail where the employer did not know about the employee's Rastafarian beliefs.

---

26 *Maistry v BBC* (2014) EWCA Civ 1116, especially at paras 6 and 12-13.

27 *Harris v NKL Automotive Ltd and Matrix Consultancy Ltd* [2007] EAT 0134/07 especially at paragraph 13.

# CHAPTER FOUR
# WHO IS PROTECTED?

It is important to understand who can bring a claim of workplace discrimination on grounds of religion or belief. It is not just employees.

Those entitled to claim are set out in Part 5 of the EA 2010, and in particular at sections 39-41. They broadly fall into the following three categories:

1. Employees[1]

2. Applicants for employment[2]

3. Contract workers[3]

## 4.1 Employees

A person in employment has a broad definition for the purposes of discrimination legislation under the EA 2010. Section 83(2)(a) of the EA 2010 provides: "Employment" means employment under a contract of employment, a contract of apprenticeship or a contract personally to do work. There are therefore three broad categories of employees:

- a contract of employment (i.e. what might be considered ordinary employees)

1 See sections 39(1), 39(4), and 40(1)(a) of the EA 2010.

2 See sections 39(1), 39(3), and 40(1)(b) of the EA 2010.

3 See section 41 of the EA 2010.

- a contract of apprenticeship (i.e. apprentices)
- a contract personally to do work (i.e. this is a more difficult category and is discussed further below).

Examples of who might be considered in employment include:

- Permanent employees
- Those on fixed term or short-term contracts
- Those in their probation periods of employment
- Apprentices
- Locums (in certain circumstances).
- Casual or seasonal workers
- Those on zero-hour contracts

*A contract personally to do work*

The first important determining factor for deciding whether someone fits the definition of "employment" under "a contract personally to do work" is whether they are *personally* required to work for an organisation (in which case they are likely employees), or whether they can use a *substitute* (in which case they are not likely to be employees).

So for example, in *Halawi v (1) WDFG UK Ltd (T/A World Duty Free) (2) Caroline South Associates*[4] the Court of Appeal held that a person working in a duty free outlet at an airport, who provided her services through a company which she had set up for that purpose, was neither an employee nor a worker within the provisions of section 83(2) of the EA 2010. She had no contract of employment and she was not required to work personally at her job but could get another person to substitute for her. Although it was rarely used, the power of substitution was not a sham.

This situation might be contrasted with a locum doctor, who has set up a limited company for tax purposes, but unquestionably has to provide personal service and cannot send in a substitute to work for him.

The second potential determining factor for deciding whether someone fits the definition of "employment" is whether or not they are an independent provider of services who are not in a relationship of subordination with the person who receives the services[5].

In *(1) Z Windle (2) F Arada v Secretary Of State For Justice*[6], W worked as an interpreter for a range of work providers, including the Courts and Tribunals Service (HMCTS). She was registered on the National Register of Public Service Interpreters. HMCTS interpreters were issued with a badge inscribed with "Tribunal Service Interpreter" as part of the security arrangements and to show that the interpreter was recognised by the service. W's services were governed by written terms and conditions. There was no guarantee of work and no obligation on her to accept work when offered. No provision

4 *Halawi v (1) WDFG UK Ltd (T/A World Duty Free) (2) Caroline South Associates* [2014] EWCA Civ 1387 (at paragraph 49).

5 See *Jivraj v Hashwani* [2011] UKSC 40 per Lord Clarke at paragraph 34-36.

6 *(1) Z Windle (2) F Arada v Secretary Of State For Justice* [2016] EWCA Civ 459 at paragraphs 8-10, 13.

was made for holiday pay, sick pay or pension. W regarded herself as self-employed and was treated as such by the Revenue. HMCTS issued a handbook for freelance interpreters which described them as self-employed and stipulated that an interpreter was not permitted to send a substitute once an assignment had been accepted. W brought proceedings based on race discrimination, alleging that she had been treated less favourably than British sign language interpreters. The tribunal, relying on *Jivraj v Hashwani* [2011] UKSC 40, held that W was not in a subordinate position to the respondent employer when providing her contractual personal services to HMCTS and was therefore not an employee under section 83(2) – notwithstanding that the she was required to provide personal service and all the other circumstances of this case. The Court of Appeal agreed.

Therefore an employee under "a contract personally to do work" must be someone contracted to "personally" perform work and be "in a relationship of subordination" with the person who receives the services.

## 4.2 Job applicants

An employer must not harass[7] a job applicant. Or discriminate[8] against him or her or victimise[9] him or her:

a) in the arrangements the employer makes for deciding to whom to offer employment

b) as to the terms on which employer offers an applicant employment

7 Section 40(1)(b) of the EA 2010

8 Section 39(1) of the EA 2010

9 Section 39(3) of the EA 2010

c) by not offering an applicant employment.

Examples of discriminating against job applicants might include:

- Not interviewing a person because of their religion or belief, or not offering them a job for this reason
- Mocking or asking inappropriate and upsetting questions about someone's religion or belief during interviews
- Offering someone a job but on less pay than you would normally offer for that position because of that person's religion or belief.

### 4.3 Former employees

In some circumstances former employees maybe protected from discrimination.

Section 108(1) of the EA 2010 provides:

"108 Relationships that have ended

(1) A person (A) must not discriminate against another (B) if—

a) the discrimination arises out of and is closely connected to a relationship which used to exist between them, and

b) conduct of a description constituting the discrimination would, if it occurred during the relationship, contravene this Act.

(2) A person (A) must not harass another (B) if—

a the harassment arises out of and is closely connected to a relationship which used to exist between them, and

b conduct of a description constituting the harassment would, if it occurred during the relationship, contravene this Act."

Example of such post-employment discrimination or harassment might include:

- Providing a discriminatory or deeply unfair reference to a former employee's new employer because they are Sikh.
- Spreading false rumours that a Muslim employee would often drink alcohol at work, knowing that the Muslim employee considered alcohol was not permitted under his religion, and this would cause him deep distress.

Section 108(1) of the EA 2010 also permits former employees to bring claims of post employment victimisation[10].

So for example if a pharmacist employed at a supermarket pharmacy raised complaints of religious discrimination, but then left his employment as a pharmacist, and some months later applied for locum work at the same supermarket but was refused this because he had previously raised discrimination complaints, that pharmacist may have a claim for victimisation.

10 *Rowstock Ltd v Jessemey* [2014] EWCA Civ 185

## 4.4 Contract workers

Section 41 of the EA 2010 also protects contract workers[11]. A "contract worker" is an individual supplied to a principal in furtherance of a contract.

A "principal" is a person who makes work available for a "contract worker". A contract worker is defined as an individual who is employed by another person, and supplied by that other person in furtherance of a contract to which the principal is a party (whether or not that other person is a party to it)[12].

Examples of contract workers might include:

- If company A contracts with company B to use B's drivers to deliver company A's goods to its customers, then those driver's may be contract workers, and company A should not discriminate against them on grounds of their religion or belief.

- An agency worker taken on to work for a few days to cover staff sickness absence may be a contract worker.

- Someone on a 3-month secondment from their law firm to an investment bank may be a contract worker.

Section 41(2) of the EA 2010 provides a principal must not, in relation to contract work, harass a contract worker. Sections 41(1) and 41(3) of the EA 2010 provide a principal must not discriminate against or victimise a contract worker—

---

11 Section 41 of the EA 2010

12 Section 41(5) of the EA 2010

a) "as to the terms on which the principal allows the worker to do the work;

b) by not allowing the worker to do, or to continue to do, the work;

c) in the way the principal affords the worker access, or by not affording the worker access, to opportunities for receiving a benefit, facility or service;

d) by subjecting the worker to any other detriment."

Examples of discrimination might include:

- Name calling or mocking someone because of their religion or belief
- Not allowing a contract worker access to the staff canteen because of their religion or belief
- Going to the employer of the contract worker and asking them to send an alternative contract worker because you do not want a contract worker of a particular religion or belief in your organisation.

## 4.5 Volunteers

Volunteers can operate under a very large variety of arrangements. From an informal arrangement involving turning up to help at a charity shop as and when you like, to a formal written arrangement for ongoing voluntary work to be personally provided in exchange for expenses, to voluntary work the purpose of which is akin to work experience or an internship. It is therefore difficult to advise with regards to volunteers and the EA 2010. Further there is very limited case law in this area clearly setting out relevant considerations.

It is generally considered that unpaid volunteers who work with charities have no protection under the EA 2010 and discrimination law[13]. This is because, as a rule, their working arrangements fall outside the definition of "employment" under section 83(2)(a) of the EA 2010. Even a paid volunteer may not necessarily be covered as an employee under EA 2010[14].

However there are some situations where certain types of volunteers may potentially be protected under the EA 2010. For example:

- where an individual has a legal contract to personally to do work (and thy are in a relationship of subordination) regardless of whether the individual is paid for the work they do[15]

- where the person is being provided vocational training by an employment service provider (i.e. practical work experience or an internship undertaken for the purposes of a person's vocational training)[16]

13 *X v Mid Sussex Citizens Advice Bureau and another* [2012] UKSC 59

14 In *Breakell v West Midland Reserve Forces' & Cadets' Association Named As Shropshire Army Cadet Force* (2011) [UKEAT/0372/10/RN] an Army Cadet Force Adult Instructor was considered a volunteer and not in "employment" as defined by s68(1) of Disability Discrimination Act 1995. In this case where there was no legal obligation to do or provide work and payment was due only if the person worked.

15 Section 83(2)(a) of the EA 2010

16 Sections 55-56 of the EA 2010

- they are special constables[17] or public officers[18]
- where an organisation uses volunteering as a way to assess a particular individual's suitability to become an employee in that organisation (i.e. the volunteering is an arrangement for deciding who to offer employment to)[19].

## 4.6 Specific occupations

Part 5 of the EA 2010 has special provisions for Police Officers (sections 42-43 of the EA 2010); Partners (sections 44-46 of the EA 2010); The Bar (sections 47-48 of the EA 2010); Office holders (sections 49-52 of the EA 2010); and so on which are not being considered in this text.

17 Sections 42-43 of the EA 2010

18 Sections 50-52 of the EA 2010

19 Section 39(1)(a)of the EA 2010

# CHAPTER FIVE
# DIRECT DISCRIMINATION

Direct discrimination is prohibited under section 13 of the EA 2010. This is perhaps the most straight-forward type of discrimination to understand. It is for cases where an employee is treated less favourably than others because of his or her religion or belief.

Examples might include:

- Not offering overtime to someone because they are Jewish
- Declining a holiday request for a Muslim employee so that they are unable to enjoy a religious festivity.
- Being rude to an employee because they are a pacifist and have a belief in pacifism.

Section 13(1) of the EA 2010 provides:

> "A person (A) discriminates against another (B) if, <u>because of</u> a protected characteristic, A treats B <u>less favourably</u> than A <u>treats or would treat others</u>."
>
> (*underlining mine*)

There are two important legislative tests to bear in mind with the above definition:

1. The less favourable treatment than a comparator test
2. The causation test

## 5.1 The less favourable treatment than a comparator test

An employee has to identify less favourable treatment and not just different treatment. As a matter of common sense you cannot complain of favourable or even more favourable treatment than others. Therefore you might not be able to complain if you were offered overtime and the chance to make extra money, even if others were not.

The test for determining what constitutes less favourable treatment is not onerous and can take into account the perceptions of the complaining employee[1].

Less favourable treatment has to be in comparison with others. So a manager who speaks rudely to most of his staff is unlikely to be discriminating against any one individual because of his or her religion. Any claim of direct discrimination against such a manager would need to be premised on the basis that a *comparator* employee would not be treated in the same way.

When bringing a claim the comparator has to be in a *materially similar position* to the complaining employee[2]. You have to compare employees fairly, there must be no material difference between the circumstances relating to each case.

By way of example if a Muslim employee complains he has been denied a holiday request for a religious celebration made one day before that celebration was taking place, and his comparator is a Buddhist employee who was granted a holiday request for a religious celebration made two months before that celebration was taking place, an employer is likely to assert that they are not in a materially

---

1 *Home Office v Saunders* [2006] ICR 318, EAT at paras 12-13.

2 See section 23 of the EA 2010

similar position. One employee made the request a day before the religious celebration, the other two months before. Ideally the Muslim employee needs to be comparing himself with another employee who gave similarly short notice for a holiday request.

The comparator employee or employees usually have to be identified in any legal claim.

- Sometimes this can be an "actual" comparator employee in a materially similar position. So imagine if there are four receptionists carrying out the same role, three are Christian and one is Sikh. Only the Sikh receptionist is not awarded a pay rise, and she believes this is because she is Sikh, her comparators will be the three Christian receptionists who are awarded a pay rise.

- Often the comparator might be a "hypothetical" comparator employee in a materially similar position. So using the example of declining a holiday request from a Muslim employee so that he cannot enjoy a religious festivity, that employee might not be able to point to another colleague who has actually been in a materially similar situation and treated differently. Such an employee can suggest that the comparator is hypothetical, for example, a hypothetical non-Muslim employee who requested holiday leave for a religious festivity at short notice.

It can be particularly difficult to determine comparators in religious discrimination claims. The following two cases illustrate the difficulties.

In the case of *Ladele v Islington LBC*[3], Ms Ladele worked as a registrar and her duties included registering marriages. When the Civil Partnership Act 2004 was introduced all London Borough of Islington registrars were required to carry out civil partnership ceremonies, shared out in roughly the same proportion as marriage duties. However, Ms Ladele was unable to reconcile her religious beliefs with the new duty and refused to carry out these ceremonies. The council commenced disciplinary proceedings threatening her with dismissal for a failure to comply with its Dignity For All policy. She complained of direct discrimination on grounds of her religion.

The Court of Appeal confirmed[4] Ms Ladele's complaint "is not that she was treated differently from others; rather it was that she was not treated differently when she ought to have been", and her complaint was "about a failure to accommodate her difference, rather than a complaint that she is being discriminated against because of that difference". It was explained it cannot constitute direct discrimination to treat all employees in precisely the same way.

The Court accepted that in this case the proper hypothetical comparator was another registrar who refused to conduct civil partnership work because of antipathy to the concept of same sex relationships but which antipathy was not connected to or based upon his or her religious belief[5].

In *Azmi v Kirklees MBC*[6] a Muslim teaching assistant was prohibited from carrying out her duties with her face covered when assisting a male teacher. Mrs Azmi claims included direct discrimination.

3 *Ladele v Islington LBC* [2009] EWCA Civ 1357

4 At para 29 of the Judgment

5 At para 39 of the Judgment

6 *Azmi v Kirklees MBC* [2007] IRLR 484, EAT

The Employment Tribunal's decision that the correct comparator was “a person, not of the Muslim religion, who covered her face for whatever reason”[7]. The EAT agreed and explained in relation to the correct comparator, “Of necessity, that must involve, in our judgment, a woman who, whether Muslim or not, for a reason other than religious belief wears a face covering”[8]. As any such comparator would have been told not to cover their face, so the treatment of Mrs Azmi was not on grounds of religion.

## 5.2 The causation test

Any alleged less favourable treatment has to be “because of” an employee’s religion or belief. This is known as the *causation* test. And so if the employer does not have knowledge of an applicant’s religion or belief they cannot (as a matter of logic) discriminate on the basis of it[9].

An employer’s religion or belief does not need to be the sole reason for the employer’s actions. But religion or belief grounds have to have “a significant influence on the outcome”[10] for direct discrimination to be made out. A "significant" influence has been defined as “an influence which is more than trivial”[11] and so is not a particularly onerous hurdle to overcome.

7 At para 52 of the Judgment

8 At paras 55-56 of the Judgment

9 For example in *Harris v NKL Automotive Ltd and Matrix Consultancy Ltd* [2007] EAT 0134/07 especially at paragraph 13, the EAT accepted that the direct discrimination claim was bound to fail where the employer did not know about the employee’s Rastafarian beliefs.

10 *Nagarajan v London Regional Transport* [2000] 1 A.C. 501 per Lord Nicholls

11 *Wong v Igen Ltd (formerly Leeds Careers Guidance)* [2005] EWCA Civ 142 (18 February 2005) at para 37

The employee's religion or belief can be the employer's conscious or subconscious reason for the less favourable treatment. Lord Nicholls in *Nagarajan v London Regional Transport*[12] explained in the context of a race discrimination claim:

> "I turn to the question of subconscious motivation. All human beings have preconceptions, beliefs, attitudes and prejudices on many subjects. It is part of our make-up. Moreover, we do not always recognise our own prejudices. Many people are unable, or unwilling, to admit even to themselves that actions of theirs may be racially motivated. An employer may genuinely believe that the reason why he rejected an applicant had nothing to do with the applicant's race. After careful and thorough investigation of a claim members of an employment tribunal may decide that the proper inference to be drawn from the evidence is that, whether the employer realised it at the time or not, race was the reason why he acted as he did. It goes without saying that in order to justify such an inference the tribunal must first make findings of primary fact from which the inference may properly be drawn.
>
> …
>
> Members of racial groups need protection from conduct driven by unrecognised prejudice as much as from conscious and deliberate discrimination."

The reality of modern workplaces is that it is rare to have a manager expressly indicate discriminatory intent. So for example you're unlikely to hear a manager tell an employee she's not getting offered a promotion because she's Jewish. That begs the question how infer-

12 *Nagarajan v London Regional Transport* [2000] 1 A.C. 501

ences are to be drawn from evidence to show an employee's religion was the reason for the employer's actions.

Looked at very simply a two-stage process is involved in such cases where unlawful direct discrimination is alleged.

- The first stage requires the employee to prove facts from which an employment tribunal could conclude, in the absence of an adequate explanation, that the employer has committed, or is to be treated as having committed, the unlawful act of discrimination against the employee.

- The second stage, which only comes into effect if the employee has proved those facts at the first stage, requires the employer to prove that it did not commit the unlawful act.

If the second stage is reached, and the employer's explanation is inadequate, inferences may be drawn from the evidence to show an employee's religion was a significant reason from the employer's actions.

So going back to the example of the Muslim employee refused holiday for a religious celebration requested one day before the celebration, suppose for a moment that he can find examples of non-Muslim employees seeking time off for religious celebrations at similarly short notice who were granted leave. That might satisfy the first stage. But at the second stage the employer might have a perfectly good explanation. For example, other employees may have asked for time off with short notice at times of the year when work was slow, but the Muslim employee asked for time off in mid-December which is the busiest time of year for that employer. Such an explanation may defeat a direct discrimination claim. But absent any such explanation, a tribunal might draw inferences that the Muslim employee's religion may have been the reason he was refused a holiday.

By way of an actual example consider the case below.

*Page v NHS Trust Development Authority*[13]

In this case the claimant had been a non-executive director of an NHS Trust which provided mental-health services. It was accepted that LGBT members of the community suffered disproportionately from mental-health problems and that there had been a lack of willingness on their part to engage with mental-health services. The Trust saw it as vital that its staff and Board should not do or say anything that could risk losing the trust of any section of the community. The claimant was a Christian who believed that it was in the best interests of a child to be brought up by a mother and father. From January 2015, he began to express his views via the press. The claimant was dismissed by the Trust and brought a claim of direct discrimination on grounds of his religion. The claim failed in the Employment Tribunal[14] which explained the Trust had taken the actions that it had not because of the claimant's religion or because he held or expressed his views as such, but because he accepted invitations to appear in the press and on national television without informing the Trust when he had been expressly asked to do so.

A clear explanation from the employer for its actions defeated the inference of direct discrimination.

---

13 *R Page v NHS Trust Development Authority* [2017] 10 WLUK 195 at paragraphs 70, 73-74.

14 At paragraphs 70, 73-74 of the Judgment

*The employee's perceived religion or belief*

Any alleged less favourable treatment has to be "because of" an employee's religion or belief or can be because of their religion or belief as "perceived" by the employer.

Therefore an employee might be directly discriminated against because of a religion or belief they are perceived to hold, or not hold, whether or not that is in fact true.

By way of example if a South Asian employee of Pakistani heritage is presumed to be Muslim by an employer, and therefore is not offered a job, it does not matter if she is in fact a Pakistani Christian. She can still bring a direct discrimination claim on grounds of the religion she is perceived to have.

The example given in the Explanatory Notes[15] to the EA 2010 is as follows:

> "If an employer rejects a job application form from a white man who he wrongly thinks is black, because the applicant has an African-sounding name, this would constitute direct race discrimination based on the employer's mistaken perception."[16]

*The employees and not the employer's religion or belief*

And importantly the discrimination has to be because of the employee's religion or belief and not the employer's religion or belief.

---

15 At Section 13 para 63 of the Notes

16 This example was referred to by the Court of Appeal in the case of *Chief Constable of Norfolk v Coffey* [2019] EWCA Civ 1061 per Underhill LJ at paragraph 11.

This point was illustrated in the case[17] of a Jewish teacher employed at a nursery run under ultra-orthodox Hasidic principles. Following a work-related social event at which the employee's boyfriend had mentioned to staff that they lived together, the employee was summoned to a meeting at which she was asked to lie by confirming that she did not cohabit. The EAT held that it was not discrimination on the grounds of religion or belief for an ultra-orthodox Jewish nursery to dismiss a teacher for refusing to lie to parents when it discovered that she was cohabiting with her boyfriend. It was explained that the nursery had acted because of its own beliefs and the employee's non-compliance with those beliefs, rather than acting because of the employee's belief, or lack of belief.

### 5.3 The employer's motive

The employer's motive is irrelevant for the purposes of a direct discrimination claim[18]. Direct discrimination claims cannot be justified in law and in general there is no defence available.

It is difficult to imagine many scenarios where there may be a good motive behind direct discrimination, but it may arise in rare cases. By way of example let us consider someone working in a restaurant kitchen being over-looked for a promotion to front-of-house because the manager assumes that the staff member will not like to work front-of-house as it involves serving alcohol which is contrary to the religious beliefs of that staff member. The well-intentioned motives of the employer are irrelevant to any direct discrimination claim which might result.

---

17 *Gan Menachem Hendon Limited v de Groen* [2019] [UKEAT/0059/18] (Swift J) at paragraphs 20-23.

18 *Amnesty International v Ahmed* | [2009] ICR 1450, e.g. at paragraph 58.

Similarly, paragraph 3.14 of The Equality Act 2010 Employment Statutory Code of Practice explains:

> "Direct discrimination is unlawful, no matter what the employer's motive or intention, and regardless of whether the less favourable treatment of the worker is conscious or unconscious. Employers may have prejudices that they do not even admit to themselves or may act out of good intentions – or simply be unaware that they are treating the worker differently because of a protected characteristic."

As Lord Nicholls explained in *Nagarajan v London Regional Transport*[19] (albeit in a race discrimination context), "Racial discrimination is not negatived by the discriminator's motive or intention or reason or purpose (the words are interchangeable in this context) in treating another person less favourably on racial grounds. In particular, if the reason why the alleged discriminator rejected the complainant's job application was racial, it matters not that his intention may have been benign. For instance, he may have believed that the applicant would not fit in, or that other employees might make the applicant's life a misery. If racial grounds were the reason for the less favourable treatment, direct discrimination… is established".

## 5.4 Direct discrimination by association

An employee might be directly discriminated against because of the religion or belief of someone they are associated with (typically a family member, but the ACAS Guide[20] suggests it may be a friend or colleague). This is known as direct discrimination by association.

19 *Nagarajan v London Regional Transport* [2000] 1 A.C. 501

20 ACAS Guidance Religion or Belief Discrimination: Key Points for the Workplace at page 6

The Explanatory Notes[21] to the EA 2010 gives the following example: "If a Muslim shopkeeper refuses to serve a Muslim woman because she is married to a Christian, this would be direct religious or belief-related discrimination on the basis of her association with her husband".

## 5.5 "Permissible" direct discrimination

Although in general there is no defence or justification to claims of direct discrimination, the EA 2010 allows direct discrimination on grounds of religion or belief in very limited circumstances related to occupational requirements. In such circumstances it may be lawful for an employer to require that employees or job applicants must have, or must not have, a particular protected characteristic. Broadly there are two categories of exceptions:

1. Occupational requirements for organised religions
2. Roles in religious organisation.

*Occupational requirements for organised religions*[22]

The Explanatory Notes[23] to the EA 2010 explain that where employment is for the purposes of an organised religion, the EA 2010 allows the employer to apply a requirement to be of a particular sex or not to be a transsexual person, or to make a requirement related to the employee's marriage or civil partnership status or sexual orientation, but only if:

21 At Section 13 para 63 of the Notes

22 Equality Act 2010, Schedule 9, Part 1, paragraph 2

23 At paras 790-793 of the Notes

- appointing a person who meets the requirement in question is a proportionate way of complying with the doctrines of the religion; or,

- because of the nature or context of the employment, employing a person who meets the requirement is a proportionate way of avoiding conflict with a significant number of the religion's followers' strongly held religious convictions.

Essentially the requirement must be crucial to the post, and not merely one of several important factors. The requirement must not be a sham or pretext. Applying the requirement must be a proportionate way of meeting either of the two criteria described above.

The Explanatory Notes[24] give the following examples:

- This exception would apply to a requirement that a Catholic priest be a man and unmarried.

- This exception is unlikely to permit a requirement that a church youth worker who primarily organises sporting activities is celibate if he is gay, but it may apply if the youth worker mainly teaches Bible classes.

- This exception would not apply to a requirement that a church accountant be celibate if he is gay.

24 At para 793 of the Notes

*Roles in religious organisations*[25]

The Explanatory Notes[26] explain that the EA 2010 allows an employer with an ethos based on religion or belief to discriminate in relation to work by applying a requirement to be of a particular religion or belief, but only if, having regard to that ethos:

- being of that religion or belief is a requirement for the work (this requirement must not be a sham or pretext); and
- applying the requirement is proportionate so as to achieve a legitimate aim.

It is for an employer to show that it has an ethos based on religion or belief.

The Explanatory Notes[27] give the following example:

- A religious organisation may wish to restrict applicants for the post of head of its organisation to those people that adhere to that faith. This is because to represent the views of that organisation accurately it is felt that the person in charge of that organisation must have an in-depth understanding of the religion's doctrines. This type of discrimination could be lawful. However, other posts that do not require this kind of in-depth understanding, such as administrative posts, should be open to all people regardless of their religion or belief.

25 Equality Act 2010, Schedule 9, Part 1, paragraph 3

26 At paras 794-796 of the Notes

27 At para 796 of the Notes

The ACAS Guide[28] gives examples of being a headteacher of a Catholic school or the imam at a mosque as roles for which there may be lawful discrimination on grounds of religion or belief under this category.

28 ACAS Guidance Religion or Belief Discrimination: Key Points for the Workplace at pages 6 and 23

# CHAPTER SIX
# INDIRECT DISCRIMINATION

Indirect discrimination is prohibited under section 19 of the EA 2010. This is arguably the most difficult area of prohibited discrimination to understand and deal with in the workplace. Indirect discrimination is where an employer on the face of it treats everyone equally but its actions unjustifiably put those of a particular religion or belief at a disadvantage.

Section 19(1)-(2) of the EA 2010 provides:

1. "A person (A) discriminates against another (B) if A applies to B a provision, criterion or practice which is discriminatory in relation to a relevant protected characteristic of B's.

2. For the purposes of subsection (1), a provision, criterion or practice is discriminatory in relation to a relevant protected characteristic of B's if—

   a) A applies, or would apply, it to persons with whom B does not share the characteristic,

   b) it puts, or would put, persons with whom B shares the characteristic at a particular disadvantage when compared with persons with whom B does not share it,

   c) it puts, or would put, B at that disadvantage, and

   d) A cannot show it to be a proportionate means of achieving a legitimate aim."

Examples of how allegations of indirect discrimination arise may include:

- The enforcement of a strict dress code which means a Christian employee who wishes to wear a cross is unable to.
- Not offering a kosher meat option in the canteen which means a Jewish employee is very limited in meal options available to her.
- Having a policy where three days notice is required for special leave (such as to attend funerals) which means a Muslim employee is denied time off to attend a funeral of a family member arranged within twenty-four hours of the death.

Paragraph 2.61 of The Equality Act 2010 Employment Statutory Code of Practice provides the following example: "An employer has a 'no headwear' policy for its staff. Unless this policy can be objectively justified, this will be indirect discrimination against Sikh men who wear the turban, Muslim women who wear a headscarf and observant Jewish men who wear a skullcap as manifestations of their religion".

There are five main limbs to bringing a claim of indirect discrimination in an employment tribunal:

1. What is the provision, criterion or practice being complained about?
2. Was the provision, criterion or practice applied generally?
3. Did the provision, criterion or practice put those who share a particular religion or belief at a particular disadvantage?

4. Did the provision, criterion or practice in fact put the complaining employee at a disadvantage?

5. Is the provision, criterion or practice justified?

Below I shall consider them in turn.

## 6.1 What is the provision, criterion or practice being complained about?

The first hurdle is identifying whether the employer is operating a provision, criterion or practice (PCP) which is alleged to be indirectly discriminatory. The PCP cannot be an ad-hoc or one-off action. The Courts explained in the case of *Gan Menachem Hendon Limited v de Groen*[1] that while it is possible for a PCP to emerge from evidence of what happened on a single occasion, there must be either direct evidence that what happened was indicative of a practice of more general application, or some evidence from which the existence of such a practice can be inferred. What is relied on must usually have something of the element of repetition about it. In this case an orthodox-Jewish school asking a Jewish teacher to lie to pupils' parents about her cohabiting with her boyfriend was not evidence of a PCP as such, but evidence of a one-off reaction to an issue that had arisen[2].

1 In *Gan Menachem Hendon Limited v de Groen* [2019] [UKEAT/0059/18] (Swift J) the EAT has held that it was not discrimination on the grounds of religion or belief for an ultra-orthodox Jewish nursery to dismiss a teacher for refusing to lie to parents when it discovered that she was cohabiting with her boyfriend. The EAT also rejected (at paras 57 and 59) the indirect discrimination claim stating that the ad hoc measure of asking the employee to lie about her domestic arrangements could not amount to a provision, criterion or practice.

2 See above

Arguably in contrast in *Pendleton v Derbyshire County Council*[3] (2016) the EAT found a teacher who was forced to choose between leaving her husband and keeping her job had suffered indirect religious discrimination. In this case a Christian teacher who believed in the sanctity of marriage, who had been dismissed following her refusal to leave her husband after he had been convicted of offences involving indecent images of children, had been indirectly discriminated against on the grounds of her religion or belief. The EAT explained the PCP was the operation of a practice of regarding as a dismissal offence a choice not to end a relationship with a person convicted of making indecent images of children and voyeurism[4] and that despite unusual facts this could amount to a policy. The Respondent might not have had to apply that policy or practice previously but the Employment Tribunal was entitled to conclude that this is how they would respond in those circumstances. The Respondent was adopting and applying a policy or practice that they would apply again should the circumstances arise. Section 19 of the EA 2010 permits an Employment Tribunal to look forward as well back[5].

Examples of a PCP in the workplace might include:

- a dress code provisions in the work uniform policy
- a qualification criterion for recruitment
- a policy on holiday leave
- the way in practice mangers allow breaks to be taken.

---

3 *Pendleton v Derbyshire County Council* (2016) IRLR 580

4 At para 35 of the Judgment

5 At paras 35-36 of the Judgment

## 6.2 Was the provision, criterion or practice applied generally?

The second hurdle is establishing whether any identified PCP is applied to persons who do not hold the same religion or belief as the employee complaining of discrimination.

So if a dress code is only applied to Christian employees (such as not being able to wear a cross) but not others employees (e.g. Sikh employees are permitted to wear a kara and Muslim employees can wear a niqab) the complaint is unlikely to be one of indirect discrimination, but of direct discrimination.

However, if the employer's uniform policy stipulated that no items of religious or other jewellery could be worn, then a Sikh employee who was not allowed to wear a kara could establish that the PCP applied to others who do not hold the same religious belief as him. In a case like this it is not necessary that the PCP was *actually* applied to others, so long as consideration is given to what its affect would have been if it had been applied[6].

## 6.3 Did the provision, criterion or practice put those who share a particular religion or belief at a particular disadvantage?

If there is a PCP and it is applied more generally, the third hurdle is establishing that such a PCP puts people who share a particular religion or belief at a particular disadvantage.

- So for example, not offering a kosher meat option in the canteen, would arguably put Jewish employees at a particular disadvantage.

6 *British Airways Plc v Starmer* [2005] IRLR 862, EAT at para 18

- A policy of not allowing religious jewellery might put Sikh employees who wish to wear a kara at a particular disadvantage.

- But a policy of not allowing more than six weeks annual leave to be taken at any one time, arguably does not put Muslims wishing to perform the Hajj or Umra pilgrimage at a particular disadvantage because the vast majority of Muslims are able perform the pilgrimage with up to four weeks annual leave.

There is no requirement that the PCP in question puts every member of the group sharing the particular protected characteristic at a disadvantage[7], as long as some members of the group are at a disadvantage.

Let us consider a case law example illustrating this point.

*Trayhorn v Secretary Of State For Justice*[8]

In this case the claimant was a Pentecostal Christian. He resigned after being given a final written warning when it was found that he had spoken about homosexuality as a sin and quoting from a passage of Corinthians Chapter 6 verses 9-11 at a Pentecostal service to a congregation of prisoners at a prison housing a large number of sex offenders. The EAT found he had not suffered direct or indirect religious discrimination when he was disciplined for failing to heed an instruction not to preach in the chapel.

---

7 *Naeem v Secretary of State for Justice* [2017] UKSC 27 at para 27

8 *Trayhorn v Secretary Of State For Justice* [2018] IRLR 502

The Employment Appeal Tribunal examined the extent to which a provision, criterion or practice had to lead to a disparate impact on a group of which the claimant was a member. Slade J explained[9], "a claim may surmount the section 19(2)(b) hurdle if... some individuals of the Claimant's religion are disadvantaged by the relevant PCP. To this extent it may be said that the threshold of section 19(2)(b) is not a high one." Therefore as long as "some" Pentecostal Christians or those of a Christian faith were put at a disadvantage by a PCP that would have sufficed. However, the Employment Tribunal had concluded (and there was no challenge to this finding) that it had not been taken to any part of the policies which put the claimant or those of a Christian faith or of the Pentecostal denomination at a disadvantage singly or as a group[10].

## 6.4 Did the provision, criterion or practice in fact put the complaining employee at a disadvantage?

The fourth hurdle is establishing whether the application of the PCP (although putting a particular religious group at a disadvantage) in fact puts the complaining employee at a disadvantage.

There may be cases where a religious group may be put to a disadvantage generally speaking but an individual employee from that group may not be himself or herself disadvantaged. For example:

- Not offering a kosher meat option in the canteen, would put Jewish employees at a particular disadvantage. But if a particular Jewish employee happily and regularly eats non-kosher meat inside and outside the workplace, then he is not at a particular disadvantage.

---

9 At para 77 of the Judgment

10 At para 79 of the Judgment

- And if in practice mangers only allow breaks to be taken inflexibly every 2 hours, this on the face of it is a PCP that puts Muslim employees at a particular disadvantage because they may wish to use their break times to pray which they are obliged to do at set times. However, if a particular Muslim employee does not pray, she is not put at a particular disadvantage, and so cannot complain about indirect discrimination.

Let us consider a case law example illustrating this point.

*Gareddu v London Underground Ltd*[11]

The employee was a practising Roman Catholic from Sardinia who lived in the UK. He and his brothers returned to their mother's home in Sardinia for five weeks in summer each year to attend religious festivals together. Between 2009 and 2014 he had taken five consecutive weeks' annual leave from work for that purpose. In 2015 his employer refused to allow him five consecutive weeks' annual leave. In his witness statement the employee asserted that he attended the same 17 festivals each year in respect of saints to whom he felt an affinity, he had done so since childhood and they were of great significance to him. However, in 2013 he had attended only nine festivals. He conceded that the festivals he attended varied from year to year.

The Employment Tribunal did not find that the asserted belief or manifestation (i.e. return to Sardinia for a period of approximately five weeks around the month of August each year to attend and participate in religious festivals with his family) can never be a genuine belief or manifestation. Its finding was simply that Mr Gareddu's

11 *Gareddu v London Underground Ltd* [2017] IRLR 404

motive for wanting that particular lengthy period off work related to his family arrangements rather than his religious beliefs.

The EAT explained[12], "In light of the Tribunal's findings of fact and conclusion that the reason for the five-week period for attending festivals in Sardinia was not the Claimant's religious belief or a manifestation of his beliefs, the Claimant could not have succeeded in establishing particular disadvantage in circumstances where it is necessary for the particular disadvantage to flow from holding or practising the religious belief in question".

### 6.5 Is the provision, criterion or practice justified?

The fifth and final hurdle, and the most difficult, is whether an employer can show that it's PCP which puts a particular religious group at a disadvantage and puts a complaining individual employee at a particular disadvantage is "a proportionate means of achieving a legitimate aim". Namely whether the employer's PCP can be justified.

The Explanatory Notes[13] to the EA 2010 provide the following example: "An observant Jewish engineer who is seeking an advanced diploma decides (even though he is sufficiently qualified to do so) not to apply to a specialist training company because it invariably undertakes the selection exercises for the relevant course on Saturdays. The company will have indirectly discriminated against the engineer unless the practice can be justified".

To establish a justification defence it is for the employer to show that when considered objectively its PCP:

12 At para 35 of the Judgment

13 At Section 19 para 81 of the Notes

1. Has a legitimate aim.
2. And is a proportionate means of achieving that legitimate aim.

*Legitimate aim*

A legitimate aim is worthy objective, a good business reason, or a compelling rationale for a policy. The ACAS Guide[14] indicates a legitimate aim may be "a good business reason, but employers should note that cost alone is unlikely to be considered sufficient".

*Proportionate means*

What is proportionate can depend on the size and resources of an employer – and so a big employer with a large workforce may be able to accommodate holidays for religious reasons better than a small employer with a very small workforce.

The ACAS Guide[15] suggests the more discriminatory the effect, the more difficult it will be to justify. It may be difficult to justify discrimination as proportionate where the same aim could be achieved without discrimination. Therefore an employer should look for and explore any alternatives to avoid discrimination.

---

14 ACAS Guidance Religion or Belief Discrimination: Key Points for the Workplace at page 8

15 ACAS Guidance Religion or Belief Discrimination: Key Points for the Workplace at page 8

## Case law examples of the justification defence

The best way to illustrate the justification defence is by reference to how it has been applied in a variety of actual cases which will be considered in some detail below.

### *City Of Oxford Bus Services Ltd v Harvey*[16]

The EAT decided that an employment tribunal had got it wrong in finding that an employer had indirectly discriminated against its employee on the grounds of his religion by adopting a working practice which required him to work on the Sabbath. The EAT explained that in determining whether the working practice was justified, the Employment Tribunal had wrongly focused on its application to the individual employee rather than looking at whether it was justified as a rule in general.

The employee bus driver was a practising Seventh Day Adventist. In accordance with his faith, he observed the Sabbath by not working from sunset on a Friday to sunset on a Saturday. However, the employer required him to work five out of seven days each week, including Fridays and Saturdays. The employee was permitted to swap shifts with his colleagues and was even removed from working Sabbath hours on a temporary basis. However, the employer who was concerned about other employees following suit refused to accommodate the employee's request on a permanent basis. The employee claimed that those working arrangements imposed a provision, criterion or practice (PCP) which placed him at a disadvantage. The Employment Tribunal accepted that the employee

16 *City Of Oxford Bus Services Ltd (T/A Oxford Bus Co) v L Harvey* [2018] 12 WLUK 667, EAT

had been put at a disadvantage by the PCP because he was genuinely unable to work on the Sabbath because of his religious belief.

It found that although the PCP had legitimate aims[17], namely ensuring efficiency, fairness to all staff, and the maintenance of a harmonious workforce, the employer had failed to demonstrate that it was a proportionate means to achieve those aims.

The EAT disagreed and explained that to be proportionate, a measure had to be both an appropriate means of achieving the legitimate aim and reasonably necessary in order to do so[18]. The EAT explained the Employment Tribunal was required to determine proportionality in terms of the PCP itself. It had recognised that any real problems to the employer arose not from granting the employee's specific request not to work during the Sabbath but from granting many such requests from other employees. It needed to balance the importance of the employer's aims against the discriminatory impact of the PCP. That balancing exercise needed to be carried out in terms of the PCP itself, not merely its application to the employee[19]. General guidance was given on carrying out the justification assessment[20].

*Trayhorn v Secretary Of State For Justice*[21]

In this case the Claimant was a Pentecostal Christian. He resigned after being given a final written warning when it was found that he had spoken about homosexuality as a sin and quoting from a passage of Corinthians Chapter 6 verses 9-11 at a Pentecostal service to a

17 See paras 17 and 19 of the Judgment

18 See para 21 of the Judgment

19 See paras 41 to 43 of the Judgment

20 See paras 21 to 28 of the Judgment

21 *Trayhorn v Secretary Of State For Justice* [2018] IRLR 502

congregation of prisoners at a prison housing a large number of sex offenders. The EAT found he had not suffered direct or indirect religious discrimination when he was disciplined for failing to heed an instruction not to preach in the chapel.

On the question of justification the EAT explained the PCPs served the legitimate aim of maintaining security and order of the prison[22].

And reasons why the PCP was considered a proportionate means of achieving that legitimate aim was because derogatory remarks regarding any specific group within the prison could be seen to legitimise misbehaviour towards them, particularly if made by someone in a position of presumed authority, such as a member of staff or someone preaching in a prison service. That legitimisation of inappropriate behaviour could risk disorder within the prison and may be seen to legitimise bullying or other mistreatment towards a group of prisoners sharing a particular characteristic[23].

*Begum v Pedagogy Auras UK Ltd*[24]

In this case the complainant, a Sunni Muslim, wore a jilbab to comply with her religious beliefs. Her jilbab was a flowing garment that covered most of her body, save for her hands and face, and reached down to at least her ankles. At an interview conducted by the nursery manager, she was offered the job. The nursery manager noted that the appellant's jilbab, as she was sitting, was covering her shoes and touching the floor. The nursery manager, considering the jilbab to be a health and safety hazard, asked the appellant if she would wear a shorter jilbab to work. The appellant contacted her

22 See para 28 of the Judgment

23 See para 91 of the Judgment

24 *Begum v Pedagogy Auras UK Ltd T/A Barley Lane Montessori Day Nursery* [2015] UKEAT/0309/13/RN

recruitment agency and refused the job as the nursery's policies were against her religious beliefs. She then brought a claim on indirect discrimination on grounds of her religion.

The employment tribunal dismissed her claim, holding that she had not been told she could not wear a jilbab of appropriate length; the nursery's provision, custom or practice that its workers could not wear garments that were a tripping hazard was not indirectly discriminatory against Muslim women as twenty-five per cent of the nursery's workforce was Muslim; and the nursery manager was sufficiently experienced to know what constituted a tripping hazard.

The EAT explained the legitimate aim was protecting the health and safety of staff and children[25].

The PCP was a proportionate means of achieving that legitimate aim given the Claimant was never instructed not to wear any particular jilbab, including that she wore at interview, only that she should not wear a garment that was a tripping hazard[26].

### *Cherfi v G4S Security Services Ltd*[27]

In this case a Muslim employee who had previously been allowed to attend Friday prayers during work was told he could no longer do so because the Respondent's client required as part of its contract with the Respondent that a specified number of officers were assigned to each site for a specified number of hours each day. A specified service provision applied to the full duration of the operating hours and therefore all security officers had to be in attendance during their

25 See para 22 of the Judgment

26 See paras 73 to 74 of the Judgment

27 *Cherfi v G4S Security Services Ltd* [2011] Eq LR 825

lunch break (for which they were paid) because they had to be available on site for the full duration of the duty.

The EAT explained an Employment Tribunal had been entitled to find that an employer had not indirectly discriminated against a Muslim employee on grounds of his religion by refusing to allow him to leave his post to attend Friday lunchtime prayers at a local mosque. Whilst that amounted to a provision, criterion or practice which placed the employee at a disadvantage it was justified.

The legitimate aim was meeting the operational needs of the employer's business in complying with a contract to deliver services[28].

The PCP was considered a proportionate means of achieving that legitimate aim having regard to the following sorts of considerations[29]:

- It was common ground that there was a prayer room available to the employee on site, though of course this did not meet his desire to attend prayers in congregation. The employee was not prevented from working on Fridays and he was not pressurised to accept work on a Saturday and Sunday. There was however work available on those days at other sites which was offered to him, so that he would not suffer financially if he chose not to work on Fridays.

- There were financial penalties involved for the employer vis a vis the client if the contract was broken. What was in issue was not only the actual financial penalty but also the danger

28 See para 45 of the Judgment

29 See paras 43 to 44 of the Judgment

of losing the contract altogether if there was a continued and persistent breach of the contract.

- There was also the financial impracticality of employing the Claimant for a part shift only, with the need to obtain another security guard for the Claimant's lunch hour and having to pay the replacement for a whole shift (whole shifts being the basis on which security guards were employed).

*Ladele v Islington LBC*[30]

The Court of Appeal held that a registrar who refused to conduct civil partnership ceremonies between same-sex couples on the grounds that to do so would violate her Christian beliefs was not discriminated against on the grounds of her religion.

The PCP in this case was to require all registrars to perform civil partnerships[31].

The employer's legitimate aim in this case was providing a service that was not merely one which was effective in terms of practicality and efficiency, but was also one which complied with their overarching policy of being "an employer and a public authority wholly committed to the promotion of equal opportunities and to requiring all its employees to act in a way which does not discriminate against others"[32].

---

30 *Ladele v Islington LBC* (2009) EWCA Civ 1357 CA

31 See para 43 of the Judgment

32 See paras 45 to 46 of the Judgment

The PCP was considered a proportionate means of achieving that legitimate aim having regard to the following sorts of considerations[33]:

- Ms Ladele was employed in a public job and was working for a public authority
- She was being required to perform a purely secular task, which was being treated as part of her job
- Her refusal to perform that task involved discriminating against gay people in the course of that job
- She was being asked to perform the task because of Islington's Dignity for All policy, whose laudable aim was to avoid, or at least minimise, discrimination both among Islington's employees, and as between Islington (and its employees) and those in the community they served
- Ms Ladele's refusal was causing offence to at least two of her gay colleagues
- Ms Ladele's objection was based on her view of marriage, which was not a core part of her religion
- The employer's requirement in no way prevented her from worshipping as she wished.

33 See para 52 of the Judgment

*Naeem v Secretary of State for Justice*[34]

This case concerned the Prison Service pay scheme for chaplains which incorporated pay progression over time related to length of service. Mr Naeem was a Muslim chaplain who argued that this placed him at a disadvantage, as the Prison Service had not employed Muslim chaplains on a salaried basis until 2002.

The Supreme Court explained, "the PCP in question is the Prison Service pay scheme for chaplains, which incorporates pay progression over time and thus pay is related to length of service"[35]. It noted, "This did put the Muslim chaplains at a particular disadvantage compared with the Christians. The appellant suffered this disadvantage and so section 19(2)(b) and (c) were satisfied. The question, therefore, is whether the respondent can justify it as "a proportionate means of achieving a legitimate aim"."[36]

It this case the justification defence was met. The legitimate aim of the PCP was "to reward loyalty and experience".[37]

Interestingly when considering the issue of proportionality it was stressed the employer was transitioning to a policy designed to eliminate the disadvantage suffered by Muslim employees. With this in mind it was stated, "But we are here concerned with a system which is in transition. The question was not whether the original pay scheme could be justified but whether the steps being taken to move towards the new system were proportionate".[38]

34 *Naeem v Secretary of State for Justice* [2017] UKSC 27

35 See para 12 of Judgment.

36 At para 42 of the Judgment

37 At para 43 of the Judgment

38 At para 47 of the Judgment

# CHAPTER SEVEN
# HARASSMENT

Simply speaking harassment is where an employee is subjected to unwanted conduct which is related to their religion or belief which causes them offence. No justification for harassment exists and no comparator exercise is needed.

Examples might include:

- Making comments about Islam being an extreme or fundamental religion which is to blame for terrorism
- Suggesting Jewish people are obsessed with money
- Mocking Hindus for worshipping animal Gods.

Section 26(1) and 26(4) of the EA 2010 provide:

1. A person (A) harasses another (B) if—
   a) A engages in <u>unwanted conduct</u> <u>related to a relevant protected characteristic</u>, and
   b) the conduct <u>has the purpose or effect</u> of—
      i. violating B's dignity, or
      ii. creating an intimidating, hostile, degrading, humiliating or offensive environment for B.

...

4. In deciding whether conduct has the effect referred to in subsection (1)(b), each of the following must be taken into account—

    a) the perception of B;

    b) the other circumstances of the case;

    c) whether it is reasonable for the conduct to have that effect."

(*underlining mine*)

There are three basic components to any claim for harassment.

1. First, to identify the unwanted conduct.

2. Second, to ask if the unwanted conduct being complained of "related" to the employee's religion or belief? Namely the causation test.

3. Thirdly, did the unwanted conduct cause offence? Namely did it have the "purpose or effect" of violating an employee's dignity, or creating an intimidating, hostile, degrading, humiliating or offensive environment for that employee.

## 7.1 Identifying unwanted conduct

In any harassment claim one has to start by identifying what was said or done which was unwanted.

Unwanted conduct can be expressed by:

- spoken words (e.g. an office joke or a flippant remark)

- in written or other communications (e.g. rude text messages or an email circulating an offensive image) or
- by conduct (e.g. an angry demeanour or threatening body language).

The ACAS Guide[1] suggests the following potential examples: bullying, nicknames, threats, intrusive and inappropriate questions, excluding someone (e.g. from meetings or events), insults, unwanted jokes, gossip and banter.

The circumstances and context in which something is said or done is relevant to whether it amounts to "unwanted conduct".

Sometimes comments which are on the face of it are offensive may not necessarily amount to unwanted conduct.

- For example if a devout Catholic employee repeatedly initiates discussion with a gay colleague employee about the Catholic church's views on same sex marriage, knowing that that colleague has strong views critical of the Catholic church on this topic, it may be difficult for the Catholic employee to later argue any comments made were unwanted. This is because the Catholic employee has deliberately and knowingly invited and initiated such discussions.
- Similarly if there is strong banter in the workplace and colourful political debate about people's beliefs in capitalism, socialism, communism, Marxism and the like, and this is regularly a two way discussion, then it may be difficult for an

1 ACAS Guidance on "Religion or belief discrimination: key points for the workplace" (August 2018) at pages 8-9

employee to argue that any comment which offended her political beliefs was unwanted conduct.

Often in harassment claims unwanted conduct will arise from “negative stereotypes” of people of certain religions or beliefs. These are usually straightforward to assess as unwanted conduct. Examples might include saying:

- Muslims smell of curry
- Socialists are reckless with other people’s money
- Sikhs are hairy and unclean.

However “positive stereotypes” can also give rise to allegations of unwanted conduct (and indeed direct discrimination). Positive stereotypes can be unwanted, first, by suggesting that there are differences between people because of their religion and beliefs. And secondly by stating positive qualities about one religion arguably you are implying other religions lack those positive qualities or have them to a lesser extent. Consider the following potential comments in the workplace based on positive stereotypes and how they might be unwanted:

- Christianity is a wonderfully modern religion shown by how it is embracing women clergy
- Muslims are such generous people because they make big donations to charity as part of their Zakkat obligations
- Buddhism focusses on spirituality in such a deep and special way like no other religion does

- Socialism is the only political system out there that aspires to treat us all equally.

There will be fewer cases where positive stereotypes are alleged to be unwanted conduct, but employers should guard against the risk such comments can present, and not simply focus on prohibiting negative stereotyping.

Let me illustrate this with a recent Employment Tribunal case.

*Lamonby v Solent University*[2]

Mr Lamonby was a 73-year old part-time lecturer in engineering at Solent University. During a meeting with his course leader, Dr Bonar, it was alleged that Mr Lamonby made offensive comments including the following remarks:

- Jewish people were "…the cleverest people in the world" and that they had a "…particular gift" for physics; and
- Germans were "good at engineering" as they were "exposed to a high level of industry from an early stage in their lives".

The Employment Tribunal explained[3], "Also while the Claimant sought to argue that his stereotyping (which it was) was positive, such 'positivity' is nonetheless potentially offensive to the recipient, firstly (using the Jewish example) because a Jew told they are good at physics, because they are a Jew, may well consider that as demeaning their personal intellectual ability/hard work. Secondly, it could also be simply grossly offensive, as the person may not be actually Jewish,

2 *Mr S Lamonby v Solent University* (Southampton): 1403818/2019

3 At para 19.2.7 of the Judgment

but feel some characteristic is being ascribed to them. Thirdly, even if they are Jewish, they might quite properly consider it none of the Claimant's business to refer to the fact and have legitimate concerns about his reasons for doing so".

## 7.2 The causation test

Secondly the unwanted conduct being complained of must be "related" to religion or belief (but not necessarily the complaining employee's religion or belief). "Related" to religion or belief is a wider category than "because" of religion or belief (which is the causation test in direct discrimination cases).

Given the definition of harassment concerns conduct "related" to religion on belief, rather than conduct "related" to the complaining employee's religion or belief, the definition of harassment will cover associative and perceived discrimination (e.g. subjecting you to unwanted conduct because you are perceived as Hindu, or you associate with Atheists).

Overt and direct comments about religion are less frequent in modern workplaces, and so you often have to determine whether more subtle comments or actions relate to religion or belief. More subtle examples might include:

- Leaving a bacon butty on the desk of a Jewish employee
- Chastising a Muslim employee for taking breaks knowing the breaks were being taken to pray
- Making jokes about wearing hats around a Sikh employee wearing a turban

- Blasphemous comments

It will not always be easy to determine whether unwanted conduct is related to religion or belief. See below an example of where unwanted comments were not considered to relate to a claimant's religion.

*Bakkali v Greater Manchester Buses (South) Limited*[4]

The employee, who was Muslim and of Moroccan origin, worked as a bus driver. In the canteen, he told a colleague (C) about a report made by a journalist who went to Syria and spoke to Islamic State (IS) fighters, quoting the journalist's opinion that they were confident and proficient fighters. Some weeks later, C asked the employee if he was "still promoting IS/Daesh". The employee was upset by that allegation and became involved in an incident with another colleague (T) in front of a canteen worker, who complained that the employee was behaving in an aggressive and threatening manner and stated that she had felt frightened. At a disciplinary meeting, it was found that the employee's behaviour had been threatening and abusive. He was summarily dismissed for gross misconduct. His claim before the tribunal was based on what C had said to him in the canteen. The tribunal concluded that, given its context, C's remark had been made because of his previous conversation with the employee and did not constitute direct discrimination. It also concluded, for the same reasons, that the remark did not relate to the employee's race or religion.

4 *Bakkali v Greater Manchester Buses (South) Limited (trading as Stage Coach Manchester)* [2018] UKEAT/0176/17, EAT

The EAT explained[5] conduct can be "related to" a relevant characteristic even if it is not "because of" that characteristic. "Related to" such a characteristic includes a wider category of conduct. A decision on whether conduct is related to such a characteristic requires a broader enquiry. "The mental processes" of the alleged harasser will be relevant to the question of whether the conduct complained of was related to a protected characteristic of the Claimant. However, such evidence from the alleged perpetrator is not essential to the determination of the issue. A tribunal will determine the complaint on the material before it including evidence of the context in which the conduct complained of took place.

The EAT explained[6] the Tribunal had found that C had made the remark because of the previous conversation he had had with the Claimant. There is no evidence that Mr Cotter made the remark because of or for a reason related to the claimant's race or religion. Therefore the claimant's harassment claim failed.

### 7.3 Did the unwanted conduct cause offence?

The third hurdle of any harassment claim is to consider whether any comments or conduct had the "purpose or effect" of violating an employee's dignity, or creating an intimidating, hostile, degrading, humiliating or offensive environment for that employee.

- A claim based on "purpose" would require an Employment Tribunal to consider the alleged harasser's motive or intention.

---

5 At para 31 of the Judgment

6 At para 35 and 39 of the Judgment

- A claim based on "effect" would not require an Employment Tribunal to consider the alleged harasser's motive or intention (which could be innocent).

As section 26(4) of the EA 2010 makes clear, in deciding if any comment had such purpose or effect not only should the employee's perception be taken into account, but all the circumstances of the case when objectively considered by a reasonable person. By way of example:

- If an employee in frustration moans "Jesus Christ!" that is not necessarily harassing a Christian employee.

- If an employee uses the proverb, "If the mountain will not come to Muhammad, then Muhammad must go to the mountain" that is not necessarily harassing a Muslim employee.

- And if an employee undertaking the lunchtime sandwich run leaves a beef sandwich on the desk of a Hindu employee (not knowing many Hindus avoid meat sourced from cows as part of their Hindu belief or that this was true for this employee) that is not necessarily harassing that Hindu employee.

The point can be further illustrated by the following interesting case law example.

*Heafield v Times Newspaper Ltd*[7]

The Employment Appeal Tribunal considered whether a newspaper editor shouting in the office for information about a story con-

7 *Heafield v Times Newspaper Ltd* (2013) Eq LR 345 (EAT)

cerning the Pope and using an expletive before the word "Pope" was harassment of a Roman Catholic colleague present in the office at the time.

H was a Roman Catholic who worked for T when it was preparing a story about the Pope. Due to a delay in producing the story, an editor (W), while in the newsroom, shouted to his colleagues: "Can anyone tell what's happening to the fucking Pope?". When there was no response, he repeated the question more loudly. H was upset and offended, raised a complaint and subsequently brought a claim for harassment on the grounds of his religious belief. An employment tribunal found that W had engaged in unwanted conduct but that to the extent that the conduct had the effect of violating H's dignity or creating an intimidating, hostile, degrading, humiliating or offensive environment for him, that was not a reasonable reaction.

The Tribunal found[8] that Mr Wilson did not know that H was a Roman Catholic; and it found that there was no anti-Catholic "purpose" in what he said. He simply wanted the article about the Pope and used bad language because he was irritated and under pressure.

The EAT explained[9] it was plainly right that, to the extent that H felt his dignity was violated or that an adverse environment had been created, that was not a reasonable reaction. People were not perfect and sometimes used bad language thoughtlessly: a reasonable person would have understood that and made allowance for it. It had been said that dignity was not necessarily violated by things said or done which were trivial or transitory, particularly if it should have been clear that any offence was unintended, and that it was important not

8 At para 9 of the Judgment

9 At para 10 of the Judgment

to encourage a culture of hypersensitivity or the imposition of legal liability in respect of every unfortunate phrase.

## 7.4 Witnessing the harassment of a work colleague by another work colleague

As the ACAS Guide[10] points out it is possible for an employee to make a complaint of harassment where they are not on the receiving end of conduct, but witness it and it has a negative impact on their dignity at work or their working environment. The employee making a complaint of harassment in this situation would not need to share the same religion or belief as the colleague being targeted.

And so a Sikh employee maybe harassed by anti-Semitic comments being directed at a Jewish colleague by a Christian manager and may be able to bring a claim under section 26 of the EA 2010. For example, the EAT in *Saini v All Saints Haque Centre*[11] upheld a complaint of discrimination by Mr Saini, who was subject to harassment because of the faith of his Hindu colleagues.

## 7.5 Harassment by a third party

Consider the situation in which a shop assistant is subject to Islamaphobic abuse because she is wearing a headscarf by a customer (as opposed to a fellow colleague). Can the employer be liable for harassment caused to its employees by a third party?

Between 2010 and 2013 there were specific provisions in section 40 of the EA 2010 dealing with when employers were liable for third

---

10 ACAS Guidance on "Religion or belief discrimination: key points for the workplace" (August 2018) at page 9

11 *Saini v All Saints Haque Centre* [2009] IRLR 74, EAT see especially paras 28-31

party discriminatory harassment of employees. However, these provisions were repealed by section 65 of the Enterprise and Regulatory Reform Act 2013.

In *Unite the Union v Nailard*[12], the Court of Appeal has provided clarification on the law of third-party harassment. The Court confirmed that, while every case turns on its own facts, an employer will generally not be liable for the harassment of an employee by a third party, unless the employer has failed to deal with the harassment in a manner that is also motivated by discrimination. For practical purposes this hugely narrows the circumstances which are likely to give rise to such claims.

12 *Unite the Union v Nailard* [2018] EWCA Civ 1203 see especially para 99

# CHAPTER EIGHT
# VICTIMISATION

Victimisation is where an employee is subjected to detriment because they have complained about discrimination on grounds of their religion or belief.

Examples might include:

- Raising a grievance about working on Sundays being inconsistent with your Christian faith, and then being sacked
- Giving evidence in an employment tribunal against your employer in support of a colleague's claim of discrimination on grounds of religion, and your employer then taking away all your overtime.

Section 27(1) of the EA 2010 provides:

> 1. "A person (A) victimises another person (B) if A <u>subjects B to a detriment</u> because—
>
>    a) B does a <u>protected act</u>, or
>
>    b) A believes that B has done, or may do, a protected act."
>
> (*underlining mine*)

There are three components that need to be established for any claim of victimisation to succeed.

1. Subjecting the employee to a detriment.

2. The protected act

3. The causation test (showing the detriment was "because" a person has done or may do a protected act).

## 8.1 Subjecting the employee to a detriment

Firstly, the employee has to be subjected to detriment. Namely, subjecting the employee to some sort of mistreatment or putting the employee at some sort of disadvantage. Detriments are widely interpreted in employment law. Examples can include:

- Being told you can no longer work from home

- Your work desk being moved so you are ostracised from others

- Being unfairly appraised or performance managed

- Having your reasonable request for annual leave declined.

## 8.2 The protected act

Secondly, the employee has to have done, or the employer believes they have done or may do, a "protected act". Section 27(2) and (3) of the EA 2010 explain what a protected act is, and it includes:

- bringing proceedings under the EA 2010 (or indeed a decision to continue with, or not abandon or settle, proceedings[1])
- giving evidence or information in connection with proceedings under the EA 2010
- doing any other thing for the purposes of or in connection with the EA 2010
- making an allegation (whether or not express) that the employer or another person has contravened the EA 2010.

So the raising of a grievance complaining about religious discrimination, pursuing a discrimination claim in the Employment Tribunal, or agreeing to provide a statement in support of a colleague who is complaining about discrimination are all likely to be considered "protected acts".

However, section 27(3) of the EA 210 provides that giving false evidence or information, or making a false allegation, is not a protected act if the evidence or information is given, or the allegation is made, in bad faith.

Interestingly the protected act need not have been against the person or the employer doing the victimising. So for example imagine a company offers a job subject to references and the reference from a former employer states that the person brought a discrimination claim previously. If as a result of this the company withdraws the job offer, or offers the job on less favourable terms (e.g. less pay), this is likely to be unlawful victimisation contrary to section 27 of the EA

1 *Aston v The Martlet Group Ltd (formerly Jim Walker & Co Ltd t/a i-Ride)* [2019] UKEAT/0274/18/BA, see especially para 72

2010[2]. This is notwithstanding that the protected act concerned the former employer and the victimisation is being carried out by a different employer or potential employer.

## 8.3 The causation test

Thirdly the complaining employee will have to show that the detriment he has been subjected to was "because of" the protected act. An Employment Tribunal will need to ask what, consciously or subconsciously, was the reason for an employer subjecting an employee to a detriment. The Tribunal will be entitled to have regard to the thought processes of the alleged victimiser.

The following case illustrates the issues that can arise with applying the causation test.

*Woods v Pasab Ltd*[3]

The claimant, a Muslim, worked for the respondent pharmacy, whose pharmacist and managing director were Sikhs. The pharmacist alleged that the claimant had made a comment that the company were 'a little Sikh club that only looked after Sikhs'. The employer considered the last remark to be racist and was very upset

---

2 In *Bouabdillah v Commerzbank AG* [2013] EqLR 651 [ET/2203106/12, 11 April 2013] (an ET decision) an employee was dismissed when her employer found out she had brought discrimination proceedings against her previous employer. She succeeded in a claim for victimisation. The employment tribunal found that it was the discriminatory nature of the litigation that caused Commerzbank problems, rather than Ms Bouabdillah's simply being a litigious "troublemaker".

3 *Woods v Pasab Ltd* (2012) EWCA Civ 1578

by it. The claimant denied making the comment, but was dismissed after a disciplinary hearing for making a racist remark[4].

The Employment Tribunal found in the claimant's favour on the grounds that the comment implied that the claimant was alleging that people who were not Sikhs were treated less favourably which was an allegation of direct discrimination under the Race Relations Act 1976 and the respondent at least suspected that the claimant had alleged less favourable treatment (and that this was a protected act).

That decision was overturned in the EAT who found that the ET had been mistaken for inferring that there had been a complaint of religious discrimination. If the comment was viewed, not as a protected act but an offensive racist comment by the respondent, then the reason for dismissal was not that the claimant had done a protected act but for making a racist remark.

The Court of Appeal agreed with the EAT that the employer had acted on the basis of the remark being racist rather than punishing her for complaining about race discrimination, and so the complaint of victimisation failed. The Court of Appeal explained that any protected act, "played no part, certainly no substantial part in the dismissal"[5].

### 8.4 Victimisation by association

It is even possible that an employee may be able to bring a victimisation claim if he has not done any protected act himself, but was victimised because of someone else's protected act, namely victimisation 'by association'.

---

4 See paras 14 to 18 and 34 of the Judgment

5 See paras 35 and 39 of the Judgment

There do not appear to be any religious discrimination cases illustrating victimisation by association, and so I refer to a case law example in the context of a race discrimination claim.

### *Thompson v London Central Bus*[6]

The claimant argued that disciplinary action taken against him by the employer was because of complaints about racism made by other members of his union. It was not the claimant's case that he had himself committed a protected act. His case was that he was associated in the mind of his employers with others who had in the past committed such acts. His case was that he had reminded his employer of those acts[7].

The employment tribunal held that victimisation "on an associative basis" (namely because of a protected act of someone else) is covered by the Equality Act 2010. However, they rejected the claimant's claim of associative victimisation because the links or associations between the claimant and the individuals who did the protected acts were so tenuous[8].

The claimant appealed and was successful before the EAT. The EAT explained that the key issue is not how far there was some association between the claimant and the person who did the protected act, but was the claimant subjected to a detriment because of the protected act[9]. And in any event the EAT explained, "It is entirely possible to conceive of a situation where an employee's membership of an organisation, which had protested about protected acts, might cause

6 *Thompson v London Central Bus Co Ltd* [2016] I.R.L.R. 9 (20 July 2015) EAT

7 See para 5 of the Judgment

8 See para 13 of the Judgment

9 See paras 23 to 25 of the Judgment

an employer to treat the employee in a detrimental way. The question is fact-sensitive"[10].

10 See para 27 of the Judgment

# CHAPTER NINE
# RELIGIOUS PREACHING

There have been a significant number of cases representing a variety of situations where employer's have taken action against employees on grounds that those employees were "pushing" or "preaching" their own religious views on to others in an inappropriate fashion. And in such cases, discrimination claims have failed against the employer.

It is likely therefore that where an employee is foisting their religious or other beliefs on colleagues in an inappropriate way, or is expressing their religious or other beliefs in a way which does or might cause upset, an employer can take action against that employee and not find themselves having discrimination findings against them. Examples might include:

- Disciplining a devout Christian employee who repeatedly offends colleagues by claiming homosexuality is a sin

- Disciplining a Muslim employee after repeated claims that she has approached other employees in the workplace and tried to convert them to Islam thereby making them uncomfortable

- Disciplining an employee who is a passionate environmental campaigner and believes in man-made climate change for making seriously derogatory comments about staff who drive cars and take flights.

Of course an employer's response to an employee pushing or preaching religion or belief should be measured and proportionate.

Any alleged inappropriate behaviour should be properly investigated. Usually an employee should be warned about any such behaviour before taking more formal disciplinary action.

In the rest of this chapter I set out some of the leading cases illustrating the problems of employees preaching or pushing their religious views and beliefs on others.

### *Chondol v Liverpool City Council*[1]

In this case C had been a social worker and was a committed Christian. The local authority dismissed him for gross professional misconduct after he had, contrary to its instructions and procedures, failed to report an assault on him by a service user, given a Bible to another service user, attempted to promote his religious beliefs to another and taken a fourth to his home outside work hours. In respect of the religious direct discrimination claim, the tribunal found that the local authority's less favourable treatment of C had not been on the ground of his religion but for improperly foisting it on service users and the treatment would have been the same regardless of what view was being promoted.

The EAT held that the tribunal's distinction between C's religious belief and his inappropriate promotion of that belief was entirely valid in principle. The comparator could be a person who, in the course of his contact with service users, inappropriately promoted any religious belief or other strong personal view[2].

1 *Chondol v Liverpool City Council* [2009] 2 WLUK 266

2 See para 23 of the Judgment

*Grace v Places For Children*[3]

G had worked as a nursery manager for P. She had been employed for less than one year and was dismissed. She was alleged to have convened an unauthorised training session at which she attempted to teach staff about the Bible.

The EAT importantly explained it would be wrong to read the case of *Chondol* as drawing a distinction between holding a religious belief and manifesting it[4]. Unjustified unfavourable treatment because an employee had manifested his or her religion could amount to unlawful discrimination[5]. However, the tribunal had been careful to say that G's treatment was because she had manifested her religion in a way which was inappropriate and which upset members of staff. Therefore, she was not subjected to less favourable treatment because of her religion.

*Drew v Walsall Healthcare NHS Trust*[6]

The claimant, a practising Christian, worked as a paediatric consultant. After regularly using Christian references in his professional communications, an internal investigation made a recommendation that he keep his personal views to himself. He raised a grievance and there then followed an independent review which concluded similarly to the previous investigation. The claimant again disagreed with the recommendations and a third investigation advised disciplinary proceedings which culminated in the claimant's dismissal. The claimant claimed that he had been discriminated against on religious

3 *Grace v Places For Children* (2013) [EAT (Mitting J, MV McArthur, P Smith) 05/11/2013]

4 See para 5 of the Judgment

5 See para 6 of the Judgment

6 *Drew v Walsall Healthcare NHS Trust* [2013] Eq LR 1051

grounds in fourteen respects, had been victimised and had been unfairly dismissed.

The Employment Tribunal rejected his claims. It explained that a proper comparator was someone whose relevant circumstances were the same as those of the claimant save for his religion, and who acted as the claimant had done but used terms relating to his own religious belief system or non-religious or atheist belief system and concluded that such a comparator would have been treated in the same way[7].

The claimant appealed. The EAT found that an employment tribunal had neither been perverse nor erred in law in concluding that an employer had not discriminated against an employee on the ground of his religion when it dismissed him for refusing to accept a recommendation to keep his religious beliefs to himself and not impose them on others[8].

*Wasteney v East London NHS Foundation Trust*[9]

In this case complaints had been made by a Muslim junior worker against the Claimant, a more senior manager who was a Christian. The complaints included the Claimant praying with the junior worker, giving a book to that worker which concerned the conversion to Christianity of a Muslim woman, and inviting her to various services and events at the Claimant's Church. The Claimant was given a final written warning, reduced on appeal to a first written warning after the Respondent investigated the complaints and had found the Claimant guilty of serious misconduct, namely the blurring of professional boundaries and the subjection of a junior colleague to improper pressure and unwanted conduct.

7 See para 58 of the Judgment

8 See paras 89 to 90 of the Judgment

9 *Wasteney v East London NHS Foundation Trust* (2016) ICR 643 (EAT)

The ET rejected the Claimant's claims of direct discrimination and harassment because of or related to her religion and she appealed.

The EAT explained that the Tribunal had concluded that the Claimant was not subjected to disciplinary process or sanction because she manifested her religious belief in voluntary and consensual exchanges with a colleague but because she subjected a subordinate to unwanted and unwelcome conduct, going substantially beyond "religious discussion", without regard to her own influential position[10].

*Trayhorn v Secretary Of State For Justice*[11]

The Claimant was a Pentecostal Christian. He resigned after being given a final written warning when it was found that he had spoken about homosexuality as a sin and quoting from a passage of Corinthians Chapter 6 verses 9-11 at a Pentecostal service to a congregation of prisoners at a prison housing a large number of sex offenders.

The EAT found he had not suffered direct or indirect religious discrimination when he was disciplined for failing to heed an instruction not to preach in the chapel[12].

10 See para 65 of the Judgment

11 *Trayhorn v Secretary Of State For Justice* [2018] IRLR 502

12 See para 31 of the Judgment

# CHAPTER TEN
# EMPLOYER'S LIABILITY FOR ITS EMPLOYEES

When an employer is vicariously liable for the actions of its employees is set out at section 109 of the EA 2010.

There can be difficulty with determining when an employer is legally responsible for the discriminatory actions of its employee's which they have not authorised, nor sanctioned, and with which they disagree or even of which they were unaware. However, the practical reality is that – except in limited circumstances – employers are usually fully liable for any discriminatory actions of any of their employees towards other colleagues.

And so the employer is fairly obviously likely liable:

- If a line manager has refused to employ a job applicant because she was Hindu
- Where a work colleague had been making offensive Islamaphobic jokes about a fellow colleague in the workplace
- The HR department's new dress code policy discriminates against a Christian employee because she is told she can no longer wear a cross.

But the employer is also potentially vicariously liable if:

- An employee discriminates against a colleague at a Christmas work party taking place away from the work premises

- An employee harasses a fellow colleague in a hotel where employees are staying for a weekend conference

- Offensive discriminatory comments are posted on social media sites, if people are only connected because of work and the comments are posted on work computers or during working hours.

Indeed social media and online activities present particular challenges to determining the liability of employers for the actions of their employees. See for example the case of *Forbes v LHR Airport Ltd*[1] discussed below.

Section 109 of the EA 2010 setting out the liability of employers and principals provides:

1. "Anything done by a person (A) in the course of A's employment must be treated as also done by the employer.

2. Anything done by an agent for a principal, with the authority of the principal, must be treated as also done by the principal.

3. It does not matter whether that thing is done with the employer's or principal's knowledge or approval.

4. In proceedings against A's employer (B) in respect of anything alleged to have been done by A in the course of A's employment it is a defence for B to show that B took all reasonable steps to prevent A—

    a) from doing that thing, or

    b) from doing anything of that description."

1 *Forbes v LHR Airport Ltd* [2019] IRLR 890, EAT

[*underlining mine*]

(For the purposes of this chapter I am not considering the relationship between agents and principals referred to in section 109(2) of the EA 2010.)

The limited circumstances in which an employer may not be liable for the actions of its employees which are discriminatory towards others are:

- When an employee discriminating is not acting "in the course of employment" (section 109(1) of the EA 2010)
- Where the statutory "reasonable steps" defence is available (section 109(4) of the EA 2010).

## 10.1 Not in the course of employment

An employer is not vicariously liable for any discriminatory act done by an employee not in the course of employment. The idea behind this provision is clear. If someone does something in their private life outside work then their employer can hardly be liable for that. A very straight-forward example is if someone gets into a verbal altercation with their neighbour (who is also a work colleague) over a fence dispute and makes anti-Semitic threats to them.

However, in practice the Courts and Tribunals have found it difficult to draw the line with what is "in the course of employment" and have interpreted the concept fairly broadly.

The Court of Appeal in *Jones v Tower Boot Co Ltd*[2] explained that whether conduct complained of was done by a person "in the course of employment", for the purposes of discrimination claims should be interpreted in the sense in which they are employed in everyday speech and not restrictively by reference to case law for establishing an employer's vicarious liability for the torts committed by an employee.

However, let us consider some of the decided cases on vicarious liability (albeit they are in different contexts and not necessarily discrimination claims) to understand what might be considered to fall in "the course of employment".

*Lister v Hesley Hall Ltd*[3]

The modern legal test is set out in this leading case which applied a "sufficient connection" test – in other words, were the wrongs of an employee that were carried out "so closely connected with the employment" that it would be fair and just to hold the employer vicariously liable[4].

In this case the owners of a children's home were held vicariously liable for the sexual abuse perpetrated by their employee the warden. The Court explained that vicarious liability can arise for unauthorised, intentional wrongdoings committed by an employee acting for his own benefit, in so far as there exists a connection between the wrongdoings and the work for which he was employed to render it within the scope of employment.

2 *Jones v Tower Boot Co Ltd* [1997] IRLR 168 at paras 32-33, 36 and 43

3 *Lister v Hesley Hall Ltd* [2001] UKHL 22

4 See paras 28, 50 and 82 of the Judgment

The Court explained that there was a sufficient connection between the work that the warden was employed to do and the abuse that he committed to render it within the scope of employment. The abuse was committed at the time, premises and during the course of the warden's care of the boys. The warden's function was to care for the boys and the fact that he performed that function in an abusive manner did not sever the connection with his employment for the purposes of vicarious liability.

*Bellman v Northampton Recruitment Ltd*[5]

The employee worked as a sales manager. The managing director was regarded as the company's directing mind, and had a very wide remit. He organised and paid for a Christmas party for staff and their partners. After the party he arranged for taxis to take some of the attendees to a nearby hotel, where they were staying at the company's expense. They all continued drinking and a work-related discussion turned to a new employee, who was said to be receiving higher pay than others. The director pointedly walked away from the discussion, before returning and summoning the remaining employees. He began to lecture them, and when challenged by the employee he punched him twice. The second punch knocked the employee to the floor where he hit his head and sustained a serious brain injury. The issue was whether the company was vicariously liable for the director's actions. The High Court found that it was not, because the hotel drinking session was entirely independent of the Christmas party and unconnected to the company's business.

On appeal the Court of Appeal disagreed[6]. It found the company was vicariously liable for the assault committed by its managing dir-

5 *Bellman v Northampton Recruitment Ltd* [2018] EWCA Civ 2214

6 At paras 25-27 of Judgment

ector on the employee. Although the assault occurred at a separate drinking session after the party, the wrongdoer was not present merely as a fellow reveller but as managing director. There was sufficient connection between the position in which he was employed and his wrongful conduct so as to make the employer liable under the principle of social justice.

In the above case an example was given of where someone would not be acting in the course of their employment[7]. Imagine a social round of golf between colleagues during which conversation turns to work. All participants are equal and attend as casual friends and golfers. In such circumstances, even if discussions turn to work and a golfer who happens to be a more senior employee assaults another golfer who is a junior colleague, looked at objectively, they have all attended as social golfers and are not acting the course of their employment.

*Sidhu v Aerospace Composite Technology Ltd*[8]

In this case the employer was not found to be vicariously liable for direct racial discrimination[9]. Mr Sidhu, was subject to a racist violent attack by a fellow employee out of hours at a racetrack, during a social event organised by the employer. The Court of Appeal explained the ET was entitled to find that such behaviour did not fall with the "course of employment". A relevant consideration was that the majority of those attending the event were friends and family rather than employees.

7 At para 28 of the Judgment

8 Sidhu v Aerospace Composite Technology Ltd [2000] IRLR 602, CA

9 At paras 22, 27 and 28 of the Judgment

*Chief Constable of the Lincolnshire Police v Stubbs*[10]

In this case Ms Stubbs was subjected to sexual harassment by a police colleague in a pub, where she had gone after her duty had ended.

On appeal the EAT found that the Employment Tribunal was entitled to find that these acts gave rise to liability on the part of employer as the harasser could be considered to be acting in the course of employment. This case illustrates how fact sensitive determination of vicarious liability can be. The EAT explained, "We concur with the findings of the industrial tribunal, that the two incidents referred to, although 'social events' away from the police station, were extensions of the workplace. Both incidents were social gatherings involving officers from work either immediately after work or for an organised leaving party. They come within the definition of course of employment"[11].

*Forbes v LHR Airport Ltd*[12]

In this case A (a colleague of the claimant) posted a picture of a golliwog on her private Facebook page with the comment 'Let's see how far he can travel before Facebook takes him off'. A shared the comment with her Facebook friends and work colleague B who showed it to the claimant. The claimant complained to the employer who disciplined A with a final warning. The claimant later brought a claim of harassment against the employer.

The Employment Tribunal rejected the claim for reasons including that the employer was not vicariously liable under section 109 of the

10 *Chief Constable of the Lincolnshire Police v Stubbs* [1999] IRLR 81, EAT

11 At para 44 of the Judgment

12 *Forbes v LHR Airport Ltd* [2019] IRLR 890, EAT

EA 2010[13]. It found at the time that the action was taken A was not in work. The sharing of the image made no reference at all to the employer or any of the employer's employees. There was nobody within the employer's employment who was mentioned in the sharing of the image. The equipment that was used for sharing the image did not belong to the employer.

The EAT agreed with the ET and explained, "In our judgment, the factors relied upon by the Tribunal in deciding that the sharing of the image by Ms Stevens was not in the course of employment were proper ones to take into account. The words 'in the course of employment' are to be understood in their ordinary and natural sense as they would be by the lay person. The lay person would not consider that the sharing of an image on a private non-work-related Facebook page, with a list of friends that largely did not include work colleagues, was an act done in the course of employment. The factors taken into account by the Tribunal also included the fact that Ms Stevens was not at work when the image was posted; that the image had not made reference to the Respondent or any of the Respondent's employees; and that she did not use the Respondent's equipment in sharing the image"[14].

The EAT further explained, "the fact that the employer considers it appropriate to take such action does not mean that the conduct in question is necessarily done in the course of employment. The employer can, for example, take action, again depending on policies, against an employee where it transpires that he or she has committed criminal acts outside employment, or acts which are otherwise considered offensive or unacceptable. An employee found to be chanting racist slogans at a football match, for example, might be regarded by an employer as engaging in conduct worthy of censure. However, no

13 At para 10 of the Judgment

14 At para 35 of the Judgment

reasonable person would regard such conduct as being done in the course of employment, unless there was shown to be some connection between attendance at the football match and employment that suggested otherwise" [15].

*Barclays Bank Plc v Various Claimants*[16]

This recent case considered whether Barclays Bank was liable for sexual assaults committed by an independent physician in the course of carrying out medical assessments on job applicants who had been successful at interview, and offered employment subject to a medical examination.

The Supreme Court explained there was no vicarious liability: "Clearly, although Dr Bates was a part-time employee of the health service, he was not at any time an employee of the Bank. Nor, viewed objectively, was he anything close to an employee. He did, of course, do work for the Bank. The Bank made the arrangements for the examinations and sent him the forms to fill in. It therefore chose the questions to which it wanted answers. But the same would be true of many other people who did work for the Bank but were clearly independent contractors, ranging from the company hired to clean its windows to the auditors hired to audit its books. Dr Bates was not paid a retainer which might have obliged him to accept a certain number of referrals from the Bank. He was paid a fee for each report. He was free to refuse an offered examination should he wish to do so. He no doubt carried his own medical liability insurance, although this may not have covered him from liability for deliberate wrongdoing. He was in business on his own account as a medical

---

15 At para 38 of the Judgment

16 *Barclays Bank Plc v Various Claimants* [2020] UKSC 13

practitioner with a portfolio of patients and clients. One of those clients was the Bank"[17].

What these cases illustrate is that where an employee discriminates against a fellow employee on grounds of their religion or belief in circumstances which are so closely connected with the employment that it would be fair and just to hold the employer vicariously liable, the employer will be vicariously liable. But where the line is drawn is far from clear and will be fact sensitive. As Choudhury J noted having reviewed the authorities in *Forbes v LHR Airport Ltd*[18]:

> "From these authorities, it can be seen that the main principle to be gleaned is that the question of whether conduct is or is not in the course of employment within the meaning of s 109 of the EqA is very much one of fact to be determined by the Tribunal having regard to all the relevant circumstances. It can also be said that the words 'in the course of employment' are to be construed in the sense in which the lay person would understand them and that there is no clear dividing line between conduct that is in the course of employment and that which is not. Each case will depend on its own particular facts."

## 10.2 Reasonable steps defence

This defence is a relatively restrictive defence and practically offers very limited protection to employers. The employer is often vicariously liable even if they are unaware of any discriminatory behaviour and even if they would disapprove of the comments made and discipline the person making the comments.

---

17 At para 28 of the Judgment

18 *Forbes v LHR Airport Ltd* [2019] IRLR 890, EAT at para 25

However, they can potentially avoid vicarious liability by showing they took "all reasonable steps" to prevent the employee doing the discriminatory act in question.

What are "all reasonable steps" is a question of fact and there is little case law guidance on this. For example, an employer might be able to argue it has taken all reasonable steps where:

- they have comprehensive and up to date anti-discrimination policies and procedures which staff are aware of
- such policies are put into practice and followed rather than simply paid lip-service to
- the employer can demonstrate that they take allegations of discrimination seriously (such as taking disciplinary action against those who discriminate)
- they give all of their staff regular training in how to prevent and deal with discrimination (and training records are kept).

# CHAPTER ELEVEN
# REMEDIES FOR RELIGION OR BELIEF DISCRIMINATION

Remedies for cases of discrimination are set out in section 124 of the EA 2010. Section 124(2) sets out the three types of remedies open to a Tribunal:

1. a declaration as to the rights of the employee and the employer in relation to the matters to which the proceedings relate

2. order the employer to pay compensation to the employee

3. make an appropriate recommendation.

A "declaration" by an Employment Tribunal would simply be the order stating that an employer has unlawfully discriminated against a complainant in the manner alleged.

Under section 124(3) of the EA 2010 "an appropriate recommendation" is "a recommendation that within a specified period the respondent takes specified steps for the purpose of obviating or reducing the adverse effect on the complainant of any matter to which the proceedings relate". For example, in an appropriate case it may be recommended that an employer should arrange equal opportunities training for employees who have acted in an unlawfully discriminatory way[1].

---

1 *Southwark London Borough v Ayton* (2003) UKEAT/0515/03 (18 September 2003, unreported)

In this chapter the focus is on the remedy of "compensation". Section 124(6) provides that the amount of compensation which may be awarded under section 124(2)(b) corresponds to the amount which could be awarded by the county court or the sheriff [in Scotland] under section 119 of the EA 2010.

Section 119 gives a very wide power to the Employment Tribunal to award damages for:

1. Any losses the County Court has power to award losses for in tort or judicial review proceedings.

2. Damages for injured feelings.

In discrimination cases there is no cap or limit on damages the Employment Tribunal is able to award. The financial consequences for an employer of a successful discrimination claim can therefore be hugely serious as discussed below.

Compensation awarded will vary depending on the circumstances of an individual case, but the general rule when deciding the level of compensation is to put the employee back into the position they would have been in had the discrimination not happened. And therefore the compensation awarded must be attributable to the specific act that has been held to constitute unlawful discrimination. If a loss has been caused by a combination of factors, including some which are not the acts of unlawful discrimination, the compensation awarded can be discounted by such percentage as reflects the appointment of that responsibility[2].

The aim in this chapter is not to carry out a detailed exploration of all potential heads of financial losses, aggravated damages, stigma

2 *Thaine v LSE* [2010] ICR 1422

damages, the grossing up of awards, interest on claims, etc, but simply to highlight the principal awards of compensation likely to result from discriminatory conduct on grounds of religion or belief.

## 11.1 Financial losses

Below are examples of cases where financial losses may be awarded:

- A Jewish employee dismissed because of his Jewish faith may claim loss of earnings for a period deemed reasonable until he is likely to find alternative similar employment, and well as any costs of finding a new job (such as travel to interviews).

- An atheist denied a promotion because she does not believe in God may claim the difference in pay between the earnings she received and the earning she ought to have received in the promoted role.

- A Hindu employer denied a company car because he was Hindu may be able to claim compensation for the extra time and cost of travel by public transport.

In practice Tribunals have a very wide discretion when awarding financial losses.

Financial losses can go beyond past and future loss of earnings (whether or not arising from a discriminatory dismissal) and can include compensation related to other workplace benefits, such as health insurance, pension losses, a failure to pay share options, or use of a company car, mobile phone or laptop.

## 11.2 Injury to feelings compensation

Irrespective of whether or not there are any financial losses, in virtually all discrimination claims compensation is awarded for injury to feelings. Discriminatory conduct is essentially regarded as inherently injuring feelings.

In *Vento v The Chief Constable of West Yorkshire Police* [2002][3] the Court of Appeal identified three "bands" of potential awards for injury to feelings in discrimination claims:

> "Employment Tribunals and those who practise in them might find it helpful if this Court were to identify three broad bands of compensation for injury to feelings, as distinct from compensation for psychiatric or similar personal injury.
>
> i. The top band should normally be between £15,000 and £25,000. Sums in this range should be awarded in the most serious cases, such as where there has been a lengthy campaign of discriminatory harassment on the ground of sex or race. This case falls within that band. Only in the most exceptional case should an award of compensation for injury to feelings exceed £25,000.
>
> ii. The middle band of between £5,000 and £15,000 should be used for serious cases, which do not merit an award in the highest band.
>
> iii. Awards of between £500 and £5,000 are appropriate for less serious cases, such as where the act of discrimination is an isolated or one-off occurrence. In general, awards of less than £500 are to be avoided altogether, as they risk being regarded

3 *Vento v The Chief Constable of West Yorkshire Police* [2002] EWCA Civ 1871 at para 65

> as so low as not to be a proper recognition of injury to feelings."

These have become known as the lower, middle and upper *Vento* bands for injury to feelings, and cases generally fall in one of these three bands.

Subsequent case law decisions have updated the *Vento* bands[4]. There then followed the Presidential Guidance on Injury to Feelings[5] ("Presidential Guidance") which at paragraph 10 uprated the *Vento* bands for claims issued on or after 11 September 2017. Thereafter annual updates to the Presidential Guidance have kept compensation updated in line with inflation. The current Presidential Guidance on *Vento* Bands Third Addendum (25 March 2020) applicable to all claims issued on or after 6 April 2019 sets the *Vento* brackets as follows:

- the lower band: £900 to £9,000
- the middle band: £9,000 to £27,000
- the upper band: £27,000 to £45,000, with the most exceptional cases capable of exceeding £45,000 of damages.

I shall illustrate the operation of the *Vento* bands with some reported cases.

---

4 See *Da'Bell v NSPCC* [2010] IRLR 19 EAT at paragraph 44 and *AA Solicitors Ltd v Majid* [2016] UKEAT/0217/15 at paragraphs 22-23.

5 Presidential Guidance 'Employment tribunal awards for injury to feelings and psychiatric injury following *De Souza v Vinci Construction (UK) Ltd* [2017] EWCA Civ 879'.

*Momand v 2 Sisters Food Group Ltd*[6]

In this case the injury to feelings award was £3,000.

The claimant, a Hygiene Supervisor, was subject to harassment relating to his Muslim religion when a colleague asked which imam he worshipped, insulted the imam by making up funny names for that imam and calling the imam a 'beggar on the streets' and laughed at the claimant. The claimant was a devout Muslim and was upset by this behaviour which was offensive to him, but it was a one-off event and was a lower *Vento* band case.

*Griffin v Surrey Rest Homes Ltd*[7]

In this case the injury to feelings award was £5,750.

The claimant was the manager of a care home who was discriminated against on the grounds of her religion (Christian) when the picture of her on her mouse mat was defaced by an employee of the respondent with a three-pronged fork and items sticking out of her hair to make her look like a devil. The claimant was frightened and distressed.

6 *Momand v 2 Sisters Food Group Ltd* (Birmingham) (Case No 1302787/2011) (30 May 2012, [2012] EqLR 841) [Harvey on Industrial Relations and Employment Law at para 1091]

7 *Griffin v Surrey Rest Homes Ltd* (Reading) (Case No 2701958/07) (9 April 2008, unreported) [Harvey on Industrial Relations and Employment Law at para 1094]

*Mrs A Dooley v Mr Lee Williams and others*[8]

In this case the injury to feelings award was £20,000.

The tribunal found that the claimant had been discriminated against (and harassed) on grounds of age and her Jewish faith by one of the employer's directors for a period of about one year. The director made a number of anti-Semitic remarks to the claimant and assigned her to handle all Jewish customers as she was of their 'tribe'. The claimant was also told that someone younger and cheaper could be hired to do her job. She was subsequently dismissed, which the tribunal found to be discriminatory. The claimant was upset and stressed by her treatment, on numerous occasions going to bed at 8pm in a tearful state after being at work all day. Her sleep patterns became interrupted and she became withdrawn. The tribunal also took into account that the claimant was dismissed from a job she had been doing for over 10 years and had lost confidence in her abilities. That she had few previous employers in her 30-year career was also taken into account.

## 11.3 Personal injury compensation

Compensation is also potentially available for any personal injury to an employee arising from discriminatory conduct. So for example, there may be a personal injury claim:

- if during a campaign of harassment a Buddhist employee is physically attacked whilst praying and falls breaking her arm

---

8 *Mrs A Dooley v Mr Lee Williams and others* (East London) (31 December 2019, unreported) [Harvey on Industrial Relations and Employment Law at paras 1106-1107]

- if being denied holiday leave to perform the pilgrimage of Hajj with family causes a Muslim employee to develop a clinical depressive disorder.

Substantial personal injury claims will usually need to be supported by medical evidence establishing a clear causative link between any discriminatory conduct and any alleged personal injury.

In a more straight-forward case involving personal injury, such as a short lived relatively minor depressive disorder, a Tribunal may factor the personal injury element into the compensation award for injury to feelings.

# CHAPTER TWELVE
# CONCLUDING REMARKS

The author hopes this text presents a useful overview of when, how, who and against whom workplace discrimination claims on grounds of religion and belief can be pursued in the employment tribunal.

Such claims present unique challenges giving rise to special considerations. It remains to be seen how employment law will continue to balance the challenges of:

- those with religious and other beliefs wishing for their employers to better accommodate them;
- the business, social, and political costs to employers of accommodating such beliefs;
- the fact that religious and other beliefs are difficult to define, are not static and can be evolving for an individual;
- an increasingly multi-cultural and multi-religious society; and
- meeting the aims of the EA 2010.

Anyone with an interest in this topic should note the lively debate about whether "beliefs" should be a protected characteristic under the EA 2010 in the same way as religion, race, gender, disability, etc.

And the author notes the thought-provoking case for reform presented by Dr James Peter Gould[1] and others who have considered the absence from the EA 2010 of a provision permitting the exercise of religious conscience by providers of employment, goods and services and employees, so that they may lawfully decline to act or offer such services without facing liability. He outlines the basis of a potential amendment to ensure a different balance – a conscience clause could be a form of reasonable accommodation (namely a provision allowing the views of religious individuals that conflict with equality law to be reasonably accommodated).

1 "*Equality Act 2010: A proposed amendment in respect of its treatment of religion*" by James Peter Gould (for the Society Of Conservative Lawyers) (October 2020).

'A Practical Guide to the Pre-Action RTA Claims Protocol for Personal Injury Lawyers' by Antonia Ford

'A Practical Guide to Neighbour Disputes and the Law' by Alexander Walsh

'A Practical Guide to Forfeiture of Leases' by Mark Shelton

'A Practical Guide to Coercive Control for Legal Practitioners and Victims' by Rachel Horman

'A Practical Guide to Rights Over Airspace and Subsoil' by Daniel Gatty

'Tackling Disclosure in the Criminal Courts – A Practitioner's Guide' by Narita Bahra QC & Don Ramble

'A Practical Guide to the Law of Driverless Cars – Second Edition' by Alex Glassbrook, Emma Northey & Scarlett Milligan

'A Practical Guide to TOLATA Claims' by Greg Williams

'Artificial Intelligence – The Practical Legal Issues' by John Buyers

'A Practical Guide to the Law of Prescription in Scotland' by Andrew Foyle

'A Practical Guide to the Construction and Rectification of Wills and Trust Instruments' by Edward Hewitt

'A Practical Guide to the Law of Bullying and Harassment in the Workplace' by Philip Hyland

'How to Be a Freelance Solicitor: A Practical Guide to the SRA-Regulated Freelance Solicitor Model' by Paul Bennett

'A Practical Guide to Prison Injury Claims' by Malcolm Johnson

'A Practical Guide to the Small Claims Track' by Dominic Bright

'A Practical Guide to Advising Clients at the Police Station' by Colin Stephen McKeown-Beaumont

'A Practical Guide to Antisocial Behaviour Injunctions' by Iain Wightwick

'Practical Mediation: A Guide for Mediators, Advocates, Advisers, Lawyers, and Students in Civil, Commercial, Business, Property, Workplace, and Employment Cases' by Jonathan Dingle with John Sephton

'The Mini-Pupillage Workbook' by David Boyle

| |
|---|
| 'A Practical Guide to Crofting Law' by Brian Inkster |
| 'A Practical Guide to Spousal Maintenance' by Liz Cowell |
| 'A Practical Guide to the Law of Domain Names and Cybersquatting' by Andrew Clemson |
| 'A Practical Guide to the Law of Gender Pay Gap Reporting' by Harini Iyengar |
| 'A Practical Guide to the Rights of Grandparents in Children Proceedings' by Stuart Barlow |
| 'NHS Whistleblowing and the Law' by Joseph England |
| 'Employment Law and the Gig Economy' by Nigel Mackay & Annie Powell |
| 'A Practical Guide to Noise Induced Hearing Loss (NIHL) Claims' by Andrew Mckie, Ian Skeate, Gareth McAloon |
| 'An Introduction to Beauty Negligence Claims – A Practical Guide for the Personal Injury Practitioner' by Greg Almond |
| 'Intercompany Agreements for Transfer Pricing Compliance' by Paul Sutton |
| 'Zen and the Art of Mediation' by Martin Plowman |
| 'A Practical Guide to the SRA Principles, Individual and Law Firm Codes of Conduct 2019 – What Every Law Firm Needs to Know' by Paul Bennett |
| 'A Practical Guide to Adoption for Family Lawyers' by Graham Pegg |
| 'A Practical Guide to Industrial Disease Claims' by Andrew Mckie & Ian Skeate |
| 'A Practical Guide to Redundancy' by Philip Hyland |
| 'A Practical Guide to Vicarious Liability' by Mariel Irvine |
| 'A Practical Guide to Applications for Landlord's Consent and Variation of Leases' by Mark Shelton |
| 'A Practical Guide to Relief from Sanctions Post-Mitchell and Denton' by Peter Causton |
| 'A Practical Guide to Equity Release for Advisors' by Paul Sams |
| 'A Practical Guide to Unlawful Eviction and Harassment' by Stephanie Lovegrove |
| 'A Practical Guide to the Law Relating to Food' by Ian Thomas |

'A Practical Guide to Financial Services Claims' by Chris Hegarty

'The Law of Houses in Multiple Occupation: A Practical Guide to HMO Proceedings' by Julian Hunt

'A Practical Guide to Unlawful Eviction and Harassment' by Stephanie Lovegrove

'A Practical Guide to Solicitor and Client Costs' by Robin Dunne

'Occupiers, Highways and Defective Premises Claims: A Practical Guide Post-Jackson – 2nd Edition' by Andrew Mckie

'A Practical Guide to Financial Ombudsman Service Claims' by Adam Temple & Robert Scrivenor

'A Practical Guide to Advising Schools on Employment Law' by Jonathan Holden

'A Practical Guide to Running Housing Disrepair and Cavity Wall Claims: 2nd Edition' by Andrew Mckie & Ian Skeate

'A Practical Guide to Holiday Sickness Claims – 2nd Edition' by Andrew Mckie & Ian Skeate

'Arguments and Tactics for Personal Injury and Clinical Negligence Claims' by Dorian Williams

'A Practical Guide to QOCS and Fundamental Dishonesty' by James Bentley

'A Practical Guide to Drone Law' by Rufus Ballaster, Andrew Firman, Eleanor Clot

'A Practical Guide to Compliance for Personal Injury Firms Working With Claims Management Companies' by Paul Bennett

'A Practical Guide to the Landlord and Tenant Act 1954: Commercial Tenancies' by Richard Hayes & David Sawtell

'A Practical Guide to Dog Law for Owners and Others' by Andrea Pitt

'RTA Allegations of Fraud in a Post-Jackson Era: The Handbook – 2nd Edition' by Andrew Mckie

'RTA Personal Injury Claims: A Practical Guide Post-Jackson' by Andrew Mckie

'On Experts: CPR35 for Lawyers and Experts' by David Boyle

'An Introduction to Personal Injury Law' by David Boyle

| |
|---|
| 'A Practical Guide to Chronic Pain Claims' by Pankaj Madan |
| 'A Practical Guide to Claims Arising from Fatal Accidents' by James Patience |
| 'A Practical Guide to Subtle Brain Injury Claims' by Pankaj Madan |

www.ingramcontent.com/pod-product-compliance
Lightning Source LLC
LaVergne TN
LVHW022101200926
848481LV00003B/1019
* 9 7 8 1 9 1 3 7 1 5 2 7 4 *